GIANTS

in the **marketplace,**

DAVIDS IN THE PEW

hubbell.rick @ gmail.com

HOW <u>ANY</u> CHRISTIAN CAN CHANGE THE WORLD

Secrets to Partnering With God, Defeating Goliaths
& Accomplishing Great Things

RICK HUBBELL

KUDU

Giants in the Marketplace, Davids in the Pew

by Rick Hubbell

Published by Kudu Publishing

Trade Paperback ISBN: 978-1-9386240-4-9
eBook ISBN: 978-1-9386240-5-6

Available in Amazon Kindle, Apple iBooks and Barnes & Noble Nook formats.

Cover Design: Martijn van Tilborgh and Bo Cable

Contents

To release destiny to an emerging generation
of Kingdom-hearted Christians.

Dedication

This book is dedicated to my late son, Nathan Richard Hubbell. May his legacy continue to burn brightly as I seek to inspire you to live boldly in love and partnership with our stunningly great God.

- John 17:4

Preface

Bitter disappointment and icy cold anger swirled inside me as I walked home from the grave – the dangerous mixture weighing down every step.

Had God failed me?

I didn't think so, yet I couldn't see how He'd come through completely on my behalf either. My usual endless supply of hopeful thoughts had disappeared. All but one. And even that <u>one</u> was hard to grasp now. You see, in the midst of those darkest days of my life, a peculiar promise had been given to me. It was a promise from God that, *every time I visited the grave, He would give me a special gift - a seed of sorts - which could somehow bring divine possibilities into this world.*

It was an odd notion, ironic even. The prospect of returning to the place that most reminded me of heartbreak and loss, as a possible way to access incredible potential, was a painful idea, yet also magnificent. (Interestingly, this same promise later became a remarkable link as to why this book may in fact help *you* experience surprising acceleration in life.)

On one hand, to risk further irritation of my freshly gaping emotional wound seemed foolish. Yet with such an extraordinary guarantee, and the cemetery only a mile from my home, maybe it would have been wise to visit daily, or at least weekly; just on the outside chance that the promise I treasured was real. But over several months, I had only made a handful of trips to the grave of my son.

Despite my few visits, I clung desperately to God's promise; it was all I had left to hang on to. Each time I visited Nathan's tombstone, a bittersweet experience awaited me. Sometimes I cried; sometimes I stood silent and just listened; often I did both alternately. *I always prayed.* And true to His promise, each time I made the journey there would come a point when I would receive an inspired idea, or a particular direction to pursue. By some means I was able to summon the faith needed to receive these mysterious gifts from heaven. I suppose it might sound strange to you, but I knew that this was God at work.

So when I left the house on that chilly February afternoon, I was expecting a miracle; an impression; *something* to be given to me by God. But that day... nothing. No impression; no inspiration; no guidance. Just cold gray skies hiding the sun. I shivered and wondered; waiting, expectant and hoping. After all, God had promised! Still......nothing. At last, reluctantly, I headed home.

And then it happened.

As I trudged along, suddenly, out of the blue, I pictured myself working on a book - and one that contained an important message; a message from someone far greater than me. Though I had never seriously considered writing a book and I certainly didn't feel like writing *anything* just then, I felt somehow as though I was *supposed* to. Even in my downcast state, the idea became more intriguing as I rolled it around in my mind. Yet it also seemed rather ridiculous: to go from being discouraged and angry one moment, to pondering such a grand project the next. Then even more suddenly, like the first strike of lightning blazing out of stormy darkness, a title flashed deep in my mind:

"Giants in the Marketplace, Davids in the Pew."

The words struck me forcefully and echoed in my heart, reverberating. They were so clear and strong that I stopped abruptly, and quickly wrote them down. They carried such impact that ordinarily I would have turned around to see who had spoken them, but I knew: "*This message was from Heaven.*" I was certain of it. How the book would come into being and shed light on the title, I wasn't sure. Exactly what the title even meant, I also didn't know. Yet in that instant it felt momentous, timely, powerful.

Despite receiving the title in such a dramatic fashion, as time went on I struggled with it. I reasoned that, at face value, "Giants in the Marketplace, Davids in the Pew" could leave a person wondering what this book is about and who it's written for. Had it been solely up to me, I would have jumped to use some hipper word than "pew" in an insecure effort to be 'relevant', or out of concern that some in the Church world might misunderstand the message: thinking it meant that people shouldn't be in Church, or something like that. (Hardly the case, as you will see.)

I might have decided that the David and Goliath theme had already been used in every possible way, and so felt the need to come up with something else. I might have wondered whether readers could relate to using slingshots and discovering their secrets, why I was inspired to depict the modern form of slingshot rather than the historical version, why there are David(s) plural, if females would answer to the name David, etc…

But thankfully, I am in partnership with God on the book and what comes of it. Though we have enjoyed working <u>together</u> throughout the process, the title came from Him alone. Good thing I didn't mess with it! You see, in my journey of writing, He revealed powerful secrets about its meaning that were *complete mysteries to me* when we started. Some of them may even hold keys to *your* future. I think you might be surprised: I still am.

Since walking home from the graveyard that day it has taken me years, lots of prayer, and countless tears – some of pain but many of joy - to explore and fashion the message contained in this book. The journey pushed me to my limit, and at times beyond where I thought my limit was. I hope it will do the same for you, in deeply worthwhile ways.

Why God gave *me* this special assignment, only He knows. **Though it sounds brash, I believe that, with His help, this book will stir some specially-prepared readers to move boldly into realms where Giants can be defeated and great things accomplished.** Perhaps *you*, my newfound friend, are one of the very people who will pick up Smooth

Stones and a Slingshot, train with them, and find yourself in the right place at exactly the right time – facing a Goliath.

If so, what will you do then? I think you'll be ready for that moment: ready to change the world. And likely, you'll do it more than once.

Foreword

Rick Hubbell and I met by one of those connections that can only be designed by God. We were in need of someone to help us brand and further develop our products, and Rick was looking for a place to serve a Kingdom-minded vision. *Trust me when I say this could have only happened by the orchestration of the Lord.* As we connected, it became obvious how gifted Rick was with words: he could take an idea and form it into a one-liner that carried deep meaning. It turns out he can also write a life-changing book: this one.

What you are holding in your hand right now is the powerful result that comes when God's gifting and man's obedience connect. It is powerful because it has been born out of both the victory and pain that accompanies one who chooses to walk closely with the Lord. Rick will walk you through some of those victories, and he is not afraid to open his heart and share the pain. For those of you who have been at this for very long, you already know that some of life's greatest victories come from seeming defeats.

Another factor that adds to this message is that it has not been written in a hurry. Rick first started talking with me about it several years ago. I have seen it grow from an idea to the valuable form you now hold. It also stood the test of a special nine-week workshop with a group of more than 30 participants who added to the validity of each idea. Many reported that the experience was first "encouraging", then "life-changing", and that "the book contains a significant, timely message for the entire body of Christ."

Because I know Rick and his multi-giftedness, I was curious which direction this project would take. Rick can inspire and he can motivate. He can instruct and he can train. He can be deeply theological and he can be very practical. So, I wondered: "where will this one take me?"

To my great pleasure; I found a full buffet. A smorgasbord of teaching mixed with drama, a full feeding on the Word, while being challenged to carry on. **I came away even more clear about and committed to the calling in my life; and I know that you will too.**

I am sure you have heard the phrase "under promise and over deliver." It is intended to make you look really good when you provide a client more than was expected. The flip side of that would be to "over promise and under deliver." So, I will admit, I was a bit concerned with Rick's style of writing that so clearly raises expectations of what is possible for you using principles in this book. Could he deliver, would I be disappointed, where was this going to take me?

Here is my conclusion after reading: *Get ready! Get ready!! Get ready!!!* This book is potent, full of useful insight, and in fact - this style of writing is just what God has ordered.

> **"Death and life are in the power of the tongue, And those who love it will eat its fruit."** *Prov. 18:21 NKJV*

> **"... God, who gives life to the dead and calls those things which do not exist as though they did."** *Rm. 4:17 NKJV*

> **"So Jesus said to them, "Because of your unbelief; for assuredly, I say to you, if you have faith as a mustard seed, you will say to this mountain, 'Move from here to there,' and it will move; and nothing will be impossible for you."** *Mt. 17:20 NKJV*

So, join me in taking God at His Word and allow Rick Hubbell to speak life to each of us, encouraging us deeper into destiny. There is surprising power in this book because it is written by one who has experienced it. As a result, **you too can call to life things that you have been dreaming**

about and have not yet seen. And if you have the faith, you can begin to speak to your mountains and watch them move.

Let me leave you with one thought: *Don't just read this one, experience it.*

Rich Marshall, Best-Selling Author
God@Work Volumes I and II

How This Book Can Help You

Dear Reader,

More is always possible with God. It's not only okay to imagine greater things in life - it's highly recommended! As you explore these pages, it is my earnest expectation that inspired dreams <u>will</u> stir inside you. Let them. You don't have to settle for ordinary...

This book exists to help you experience breakthroughs in your life that you deeply desire, but that remain frustratingly out of reach. In it, may you mysteriously find a path to live boldly in partnership with God, defeat Goliaths, and accomplish great things in the everyday world.

In Christ,

Rick Hubbell

P.S. As you read, no matter what great dreams are in your heart or what challenges you may be facing, I pray that God will touch your life so powerfully that it amazes you. I hope you find an on-ramp deeper into your Destiny from <u>wherever</u> you are today - *clarity* for your next steps, *strength* for the road ahead, and *propulsion* that helps you surge forward. Such a bold aim is pure nonsense without God's help, so let's ask Him for it. *Heavenly Father, we humbly request your amazingly powerful help for every one of us, every time we pick up this book, in between those times, and beyond.*

Chapter 1
Getting Started

An amazing opportunity stands right in front of you: life. Yours.

You, my new friend, are an original masterpiece filled with precious ingredients and loaded with potential. Such unique gifts and personality are part of the reason why no one else on earth can do what you can. You are definitely not a slave, a robot, or a cheap copy - and certainly not evolved slime. You are incredible; a champion. What's more, you probably know all that...

So the natural question is, 'With <u>all that</u> going for you, how's it going with <u>all that</u>?'

Better in some areas than others, right? After all, as life happens we all settle in and make adjustments. Who wouldn't? But maybe, like me, you're not quite satisfied with that. Something inside tells you it's not wrong to dream about a greater purpose and long to see it fulfilled - even though some parts may seem far away or even impossible.

But you haven't given up yet, right? ...Of course not. Neither have I - so let's forge ahead together.

As we go, you should find keys that unlock doors you previously could not open. Some of the keys are in plain sight and others lie hidden.

This book is in your hands for a reason. As we go, you should find keys that unlock doors you previously could not open, along your Road of Destiny. Some of the keys are in plain sight, while others lie hidden.

Yet keys alone won't get you there, even though they help. God is the one and only true GPS of Destiny. And though sometimes you might find it hard to believe that your Destiny is out there, I am fully persuaded that yours is incredible, and closer than you might guess.

Think about it: *from wherever you are, <u>even</u> <u>one</u> <u>next</u> <u>step</u> in the right direction* - **just one!** - **puts you on course.** String several steps together and you've really got something going. It's truly that simple.

So, if you are ready to not only *discover* the way that leads deeper into your Destiny - but *step right into it* once you locate the path - you're in for an exciting journey.

Beyond Ordinary

You've no doubt heard talk about 'going beyond ordinary' into something more: a life that matters, one filled with impact and Destiny. You wake up every day and your life means something, not just to you, but to those you touch as only you can. Everyone wants a life like that.

Maybe you have reached out to grab hold of such a life here and there, to enter into it the way you dream, the way you secretly hope is possible. Perhaps you've caught a glimpse or two. But despite plenty of desire and information, so far you still haven't found the way.

At some point the idea of being here for a purpose caught your attention, eh? Mine too. Well, to *discover* your purpose is one thing – to *fulfill* it, quite another. But you *do* have to start by knowing where you are headed. So if you're like most people, you set out to learn more about why God put you here. The funny part is, with so much hoopla in recent years over learning *about* one's purpose, the study itself can divert you from the playing field of your own life. You end up doing more thinking about the future than moving toward it.

It happened to me.

There I sat on the sidelines, sipping a soothing combination of books and messages, wondering if I could ever slay a real Giant should one appear. *Where was my trusty slingshot anyway? Did I know how to use one?* In fact - *Where are the Giants?*

I did some okay things now and then, but they rarely seemed to be ones that made the kind of major difference I felt capable of. *The daring exploits I dreamt about always seemed to be in some future I hadn't gotten to yet.* So I kept doing all the normal things that good Christians are 'supposed' to - for years. A lot of it made sense. Yet some of it didn't, and something was definitely missing.

If you're anything like me, after a while you realize that business-as-usual will just plod along mindlessly forever. So you need to eject the autopilot. After all, that guy doesn't know the way to your Destiny. Yet once you dismiss him, how will you find the heading that transforms your everyday life into what you dream it could be? And besides, I know you've been disappointed a few times by people who raised your hopes, so you may hesitate to let your defenses down so we can really go to work.

No problem, my friend, I understand. Take heart, because your potential is simply what you haven't done yet, but could. *And still can.*

I am going to share with you what I found out and what shook me so incredibly that I'll never be the same. It awoke me to my future, and more importantly – to yours.

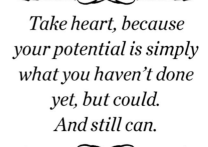

Take heart, because your potential is simply what you haven't done yet, but could. And still can.

3

A Game-Changing Weapon

One day I came across something that looked quite ordinary, but turned out to be more valuable than I ever imagined. When I first saw it, it didn't look like much. Most days I'd have kept right on walking. But that day I picked it up and started to wonder how it worked. It took time, but I began to see that this plain-looking Slingshot held some powerful secrets.

You can even slay Goliaths with it.

It's so effective and versatile that it often helps you do what otherwise would be virtually impossible. 'Unlikely' heroes often choose one. So if you dream big, yet therefore sometimes feel like a long shot, and you want to learn how a genuine underdog can truly prevail - get ready to grab a Slingshot. Few know how to use one - which brings me to a sincere request. *I need your help.* You see, while I do plan to slay more Giants, there are only so many I can personally defeat.

But with your help, *David*, we will take MANY down.

What to Expect & How to Unlock the Secrets of This Book

As we go, please let God strengthen you. Words alone will not be enough. While you learn to understand mysteries about Giants such as what they look like, how they act, why they go mostly unnoticed - and how to defeat some you may be facing - you'll find the information stunningly practical. Some of the greatest lessons will teach you how to identify the right Smooth Stones, and *The Secrets of the Slingshot*: four strategies that, when used together properly, will help you accelerate results in almost anything you do. What you learn can be applied personally as well as in larger contexts: groups, startups, non-profit organizations, businesses, and many other kinds of initiatives.

The book is divided into three main sections which should be read in order (though later you may want to reference certain parts as desired, once you have completed it the first time): *Section 1 - Partnering with God; Section 2 - Defeating Goliaths;* and *Section 3 - Accomplishing Great Things in the Everyday World.*

Along the way, you'll also discover important keys to your *True Identity* and your *Special Assignment,* and

By taking your time, you are likely to have experiences beyond what is written; personal moments with God. Those are more important than what is in these pages. So please be ready to pause and listen.

other precious secrets such as: *How to Partner with God.* There will also be a few surprises. In the end, you'll find out why certain people beat seemingly impossible odds not just once but repeatedly, accomplishing great things; and why (sadly) most people don't, even though they could.

There's no need to *rush* through. In fact, please don't. If you move too fast you will almost certainly miss something intended for you. Also, by taking your time, you are likely to have experiences beyond what is written: personal moments with God. Those are more important than what is in these pages. So please be ready to pause and listen to what He has to say to you. When possible, read while you have room to wonder and explore ideas and possibilities, and to pray now and then if you'd like.

In some places *Giants in the Marketplace* reads like a story, in others a guidebook, or even a personal note of encouragement. To get the most out of the journey, it's important to let your imagination carry you freely between all forms. You have nothing to lose by allowing that, and plenty to gain.

When you arrive at the end of the book, you'll be poised for

5

breakthrough. However, only when you step out with the new knowledge you have gained will you enter into it. But don't worry: when the time comes you'll be ready.

So today, whether you feel right on track or behind the curve, it's what you'll do next (and after that) which matters more. Your future can begin to unfold in an astounding, new direction – and it will - as you and I learn to partner with God in the everyday world. We'll defeat Goliaths and accomplish great things.

Now let's start moving deeper into your greater possibilities with God…

Chapter 1
Key Takeaways & Giant Slayer Tips

- Life is an amazing opportunity; yours is filled with potential & *you* can **accomplish great things**.

- It's not wrong to dream about greater purpose and long to see it fulfilled. **Keep dreaming**, but also take action.

- Many of the keys inside are in plain sight, but *some lie hidden*. **Take your time**.

- Living life on auto-pilot - even 'Christian' auto-pilot - can cause you to miss your Destiny. **Eject the auto-pilot**.

- Some of the best moments you'll have while reading this book are **when you put it down**: to dream, reflect, listen, and imagine with God.

SECTION I
Partnering With God

With the right partner, any Christian can do truly extraordinary things.

- **Discover Giant Secrets and the Importance of Base Camp**
- **Pass a Crucial Life Test Which Many Christians Fail**
- **Defeat 4 Challenges Which Block the Way to Partnership**
- **Clarify Your *True Identity & Special Assignment***
- **Learn Where to Find *The Great Entrance to Your Destiny***
- **Enter the Most Fulfilling Partnership on Earth**

All this, and more, is next. The journey begins…

Chapter 2
A Shocking Discovery:
The Land of Giants

The earth is the Lord's, and all it contains… *Ps. 24:1 NASB*

It's no accident you are reading this book, David, and that the idea of slaying Giants intrigues you. Perhaps that's because deep down you believe it might actually be possible - *and something about that excites you!* But it also begs the question: *What Giants?* And if indeed there are any: *Where are they?*

To pursue this quest of becoming a Giant Slayer means that we'll need to look into a matter which might shake you up and raise your doubts at first. However, getting to the bottom of this is potentially life-changing.

Are you ready?

Your chances of finding *anything*, let alone a Giant, when you neither know what to look for <u>nor</u> where to find it, are pretty slim. But if you know at least one or the other, you've got a shot.

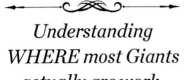

Understanding WHERE most Giants actually are working, unlocks a door of opportunities to the life you have been dreaming of, a place where you can really make a difference.

The first secret to becoming a Giant Slayer is in plain sight, but it's so ordinary looking, it's easy to miss. Most believers unknowingly pass right by. It is a key to *where* Giants roam. For many, this truth opens a door to the life they have been dreaming of but couldn't seem to find, a place where they can really make a difference.

If you want to discover it, sit up on the edge of your seat and turn your ear this way. I am going to tell you a Giant secret. It's simply this:

*Many of the fiercest Giants are **not** where most Christians think they are.*

Bumping into Giants

I was a full-time associate pastor at a thriving local church. A number of city officials, prominent citizens, and business people were going to meet to discuss the future of our city, and I wanted to participate.

As the day approached my excitement grew. "Shaping the future," I thought, "what a perfect place for a Kingdom citizen to be involved!"

"I'm interested in the future of our city," I reasoned, "therefore God must be even more interested than I am; this is going to be great!"

On my way to the meeting, though, an uneasy feeling grew in my stomach. Eventually it crept over the rest of my body until there was a lump in my throat and my mouth tasted chalky. I felt surprisingly anxious and I started second-guessing my decision to attend. It was very unsettling, because just minutes earlier I had been quite excited about being part of such an important event.

"What was I thinking? Surely no other pastors will be there."

"I must be crazy to want to be part of this group!"

"Surely I have something more important to be doing!"

By the time I arrived and parked the car, I was so unsure of myself that I almost turned right around and drove home. Finally I clenched my teeth, grabbed my planner, and opened the car door. Walking across the parking lot, I had no idea what was about to hit me.

As I looked up at the large, multi-story building, suddenly a cluster of the major forces at work in a city (and what a significant task it is to lead one!) swirled together in my mind: the government, the businesses, the schools, the poor, the economy, the enforcement of the law, the development of technology, the influence of the extremely rich, the spiritual community, healthcare, the arts & entertainment, the criminal element, etc…

Very strangely, it felt to me then as if these groups were somehow actual *forces* or *entities* of some sort, and that they were all looking down on me from somewhere in that big building. And they were laughing at me, mocking: "Silly Associate Pastor, what are *you* doing here? You and your Faith belong back at church!"

Suddenly the scene in my mind shifted, and I saw myself sitting behind the desk of the Mayor. As I sorted through all the responsibilities of the mayor, I pictured some aspects of the city running smoothly, while others were harder to get a handle on.

"In his shoes, how would I manage all those arenas?"

What startled me was that *certain problems seemed virtually impossible to change;* as if no matter what solutions I were to try, those problems would simply never budge. It was as if some larger, invisible force was at work behind those problems, locking out hope and limiting possibilities. I couldn't see what this force was, but somehow I knew it was indeed there. It felt dark and impenetrable.

Though the whole weird experience caught me *totally* off guard, it was surprisingly clear to me which city problems were connected to the 'darkness'. As I thought about tangling with those problems, I shuddered impulsively, and felt myself backing away. If I were in charge, whatever plan I'd had, I would need to adjust it and avoid those areas! No sense in beating my head against a wall!

"It's probably always been this way; everybody has to work around *some* seemingly unsolvable issues. For that matter, I suppose that's just the way it is when you are in charge of a city, or anything important in the everyday world. Focus on what I can actually change and just leave the rest; that's wisdom, right?"

Suddenly I felt an actual sensation of weight on my shoulders, pressing me down. It felt like a Giant invisible force was gradually squishing me. "What is happening?!" I thought; "I must be imagining things!" But the sensation grew until I literally hunched forward, grimacing and scrunching my fists. I tried to resist and push back, but the weight kept on coming. Overwhelmed physically and emotionally, I felt very small and terribly out of place. "*Surely I am not supposed to be here; definitely not!*"

Or was I?

No sooner had I turned away to avoid going in and to alleviate the pressure, when a different feeling rose up inside me. In a split second, in my mind's eye, I was thrust into the ancient story of David and Goliath - except that there were *many* Giants. And David…was ME.

Bizarre! And, quite frankly, alarming.

It was as if that old tale came alive for just an instant in that parking lot. All those forces in the city suddenly became real Giants - yet simultaneously, each one seemed like a potential target! Was I losing my mind? I searched my memory to discover when I had last even read any account of David and Goliath. It had been a while. In fact, I had a hard time remembering when I had even last *thought* about the story.

"What in the world is going on?" I thought; stunned and shaken, I tried to steady myself. But just then, out of nowhere, an incredible feeling of heroic confidence swept over me – a confidence so strong it was like suddenly discovering that I had superpowers! In one determined motion, I wheeled around and walked boldly into the building – with my shoulders back and my head held high. The courage and sense of purpose inside me were incredible!

Then moments later it was gone, and I felt normal again, except for my racing heart. "What was *that*," I wondered, "an anxiety attack?"

But an anxiety attack made no sense. I already knew exactly what an attack of 'nerves' felt like, from my experiences as a public speaker. *This* had been *completely* different! It was far more detailed and intense, so that in just a few seconds I seemed to have learned an entire series of lessons. Stranger still, there seemed to be an order to it all: the flow of the 'scenes' had felt orchestrated.

"Oh well, whatever," I thought. I kept walking, shaking my head, blinking a few times as I stepped into the elevator. Ballooning my lips and cheeks, I exhaled. "Time to compose myself," I thought. After a brief, uneventful meeting, I met a few interesting people who wanted my business card and to talk about what they were doing. There were no other pastors in the room. Most of the attendees looked curiously at me when I told them I was one.

Over a decade later, I had no idea that I would be sharing this surprising occurrence with anyone. I'd largely shelved the memory, until in the process of writing this book the Lord reminded me of it.

But in fact, David, discovering the <u>location</u> *of certain Giants,* what they look like and what they are up to - *why* they're there - is vital to your Special Assignment on Earth.

And that's just the beginning.

Base Camp & Beyond

Now from what most Christians have been taught and what we see other Christians doing, you might think that what God mainly cares about is what is currently going on in the sphere most people consider 'ministry': you know - church services, missions work, special non-profit initiatives, and outreach.

Those things are important, of course. But God has other plans too:

what about the rest of Creation? I don't simply mean geographically, but other sectors beyond the church world. This brings us to a precious secret for Giant Slayers; guard this one.

David, when you come to see that in one sense a local church is more like a wonderful **Base Camp**, everything changes. A Base Camp equips, organizes, and deploys its key resources toward a variety of strategic targets *beyond* camp. Therefore, a Base Camp that tried to convince all people that everyone's main objectives should be *inside* camp would be most un-strategic. If everybody sought to invest their entire lives at the base alone, it would go from being highly effective to bloated, homogenous, and lethargic. A properly functioning Base Camp is a wonderful place, and all servicemen and women need to return there regularly to be revitalized, to receive further training, and to contribute (and for even more) – *but it's supposed to be far more like a launching pad for Giant Slayers than a warehouse of potential.*

Only a small fraction of people work at Base Camp full-time; the rest are sent out into other parts of society on important Special Assignments!

Does this mean, if you don't happen to be one of the people called to lead or serve at Base Camp full-time, that you are a second-class Kingdom citizen? No way. If that were true, there would be little hope, and even less purpose, for the rest of *everything* going on all over Creation. But God is far more imaginative than that!

Besides, David, *doesn't the entire earth belong to God, not just certain parts?*

"The earth is the Lord's, and all it contains..." *Ps 24:1 NASB*

That's what the Inspired Guidebook says. <u>Every single dimension of life and society on the earth is included in those few words; it *all* belongs to Him.</u>

Yet if our God is so wonderful and so powerful and owns it all, then why are so many things in the world so messed up? And what's stopping His people in so many walks of life from encountering Him more? *If His people know so much, and we are supposedly connected with such a great God, why do surprisingly few of us make the impact in our lives that we feel called to?* After all, one would think the deck would be stacked in our favor.

Let's just say there are a lot of people who believe that the more spiritual they become, the more time they should spend at Base Camp and less time in the everyday world. But the idea that *the only way to please God is to do less in the everyday world and more at Base Camp* is like kryptonite to a would-be Giant Slayer. Don't fall for that one. Most Giants aren't at Base Camp!

"Giants in the Marketplace & the Importance of Base Camp"

Giants in the Marketplace!

So where are they? Surely I'm not saying there are Giants affecting <u>your</u> everyday life in the everyday world, am I? What could all this possibly have to do with you?

A lot.

You see, David, if there truly are Giants in the Land, at loose in the everyday world, wouldn't it be smart to learn a little more about them? The question would become this: who would dare take one on, and how would they go about it? "Not me!" you might think. Why you're just an ordinary worker, an everyday professional, a stay-at-home mom, a salesperson or local business owner or retired grandparent. You're an artist or a teacher or a public servant. In fact, why should you even care about Giants or battles or slingshots or any of this stuff? It's pure nonsense, right?

Hold on. Remember my strange experience in the parking lot, right before the city planning meeting?

What if it's *really true* that not only ARE there Giants at work in the everyday world, but *if you learn to open your eyes in a different way, you will see them?* What if it's really true that, if you want to accomplish great things in your life as a Christian, not understanding this truth may have been holding you back?

You may never have given it much thought. Why would you? It could seem like an outrageous idea: *Giants in the Marketplace*?!? Hah. What kind of Giants? What would Giants be doing in the Marketplace?! But when it actually sinks in - I mean settles right down inside your heart and goes 'Bing!' - then lots of things start to make more sense. *And Giants get nervous.*

You see, David, it really, *really* matters.

It's revolutionary.

Especially because 'the marketplace' doesn't simply mean where 'business' happens. It means the entire everyday world beyond Base Camp, **where *most* people live *most* of their lives**. Places where we work and dream everyday: schools, businesses, shopping malls, political offices, baseball parks, movie studios, and around the dinner table – that's what I mean by 'marketplace'.

And the Giants are not 'somewhere else'. They are right here: where you work, in places that shape society and influence it. They are in problems that confront our world.

Yet we miss them, dismiss them, or leave the job to someone else, not realizing how these Giants affect our lives. It's tempting to ignore them; it really is. But those attitudes must come to an end - and they will - as you and I catch a new vision to step out into the everyday world, equipped by God.

When that happens - Giants beware!

With your eyes truly open, as you go to work, or school, or choose a certain career, or are simply out and about - *suddenly you will see that there are Giants in the Land who don't belong there, that you didn't see before.* They are right in places where you thought you were just going about 'normal life', minding your own business like a 'good Christian'! But you can't ignore them anymore. You can't let the injustice of those bullies rule the day. They oppose God and His Kingdom, and they are sabotaging people's lives.

And when you recognize these thugs on your home turf, it's no longer just someone else's job; you won't stand for it. So you start looking for a Slingshot.

Good, David. Very good!

A Juicy Secret

> "For the creation waits with eager longing for the revealing of the sons of God." *Rom. 8:19 ESV*

Before we move on, I want to share an incredible secret with you.

You, David, are part of a generation of believers who are waking up to their true potential and calling in all of life; a group of leaders so incredible the world has never seen anything like you.

You have inspired dreams down inside you that haven't taken place yet, but they will. You won't be lured into parking your Faith at Base Camp and leaving Giants to run the rest of society. Together, we're going to face the Giants where we have been letting them run around largely unopposed for far too long – in the marketplace!

It's up to us, David. Can you see how this will make all the difference in the

The Giants are not 'somewhere else'. They are right here! They are in centers of influence: the places that shape society. They are in problems that confront our world.

19

Chapter 2

Key Takeaways & Giant Slayer Tips

- God **wants you to excel in life** and **He will help you** do so.

- *Many of the fiercest Giants are **not** where most Christians think they are.*

- **Base Camp** - that which is traditionally considered local church and 'ministry', is not actually the place where many of the most strategic spiritual battles are won and lost. Base Camp is a place to equip Kingdom citizens, strengthen them, reveal strategy, and launch them into Destiny – not a place to consume their lives.

- **Giants Slayers need Base Camp and Base Camp needs Giant Slayers.**

- There are **Giants in the Marketplace**, the everyday world. With some training you will learn how to spot and defeat them.

- You are part of an **emerging generation of Kingdom leaders** unlike any the world has ever seen.

Chapter 3
The Giant Slayer's First Test

"His master commended him: 'Good work! You did your job well. From now on be my partner." *Matt. 25:23 MSG*

Have you ever wondered what role you actually play in life? Most people do. But how much good can you really do with your efforts anyway, you might also wonder. It would be easier to simply sit back and wait to see how everything turns out; just mind your own business and get through life, since you know that, as a Kingdom citizen, you are on the winning side. After all, *"whatever will be, will be,"* right?

What about you, David?

To make a genuine difference, to slay real Giants (like those we caught a glimpse of in the previous chapter), can seem like awfully dangerous work. Not everyone succeeds; that's a fact. However, despite any doubts you might have, and even though you might not see this yet, there is tremendous greatness inside you, David. I want all of it, every drop, to come forth. I want you to experience the fullness of life that you yearn for deep down.

But there is a fork in the road of your life, and to release the full measure of grace and fulfillment your life can deliver, you can't go the way everyone else does. Scores of people go left, down the supposedly 'safe', 'easy', broad path; Giant Slayers go right - *toward* the daring exploits and obvious dangers. If you want to go that way, there's a test waiting: a crucial next step. To achieve your highest God-given potential, you'll have to pass this one. It may seem intimidating at first, yet I'm certain you can do it if you're willing.

Here we are at the crossroads. Which way are you going to go? I'll give you a minute…

Excellent choice! To the right it is then: the path of Giant Slayers!

The test is whether or not you will *fully* embrace a mysterious gift that God has given to you: the power to make choices and take action, and to *embrace the responsibility for your choices in life*. It's impossible to defeat Goliaths or accomplish great things until you do. You may believe that you have already done this. Even so, this test deceives many, so let's tackle it together right now.

Embrace personal responsibility. Here's how…

You can't live passively, simply hoping for things to change for the better. They probably won't. And you can't keep blaming others for your current situation. Don't simply count on them to do what you think or hope they should. Life doesn't happen *to* you unless *you* allow that; your life flows out of *your* decisions. *You decide* to take certain actions, and then you take them. This doesn't mean some matters are not beyond your control; and yes, others' choices can affect you. Nonetheless, there are things *you* are responsible for. Those are the ones we're talking about. *Your* choices and actions make a profound difference.

The Remarkable Inventor

I once worked with a Remarkable Inventor.[1] This promising guy was a highly intelligent, middle-aged man we'll call Billy. Billy was brimming with good ideas, and had a track record of modest success in his field. Throughout his career, he demonstrated great skill and the ability to creatively engineer all kinds of things.

Up to that point in his life's work, like many people, Billy had worked mostly as an employee. However, things were changing; now Billy wanted to launch out on his own. But taking the right steps in this completely new direction wasn't easy. With what he hoped was an inspired, multi-million dollar idea in hand, he decided to pursue its development full-time. Working with a well-rounded group of others, he shared his vision and worked on moving things along. He engaged an attorney and an assortment of other professionals for advice.

To date, though, not much had come of the effort, other than some drawings, rough prototype concepts, and an exciting pitch. That's when we met. I really liked Billy, right from the start. Though his manner was somewhat abrupt, I could tell that God wanted to do great things with him. It was fun to listen to Billy share his ideas – he was passion on display once he got talking!

As we talked in person that first time, Billy spoke of some family problems he had, and I felt for him. As he told his story, Billy was clear why his big breakthrough hadn't appeared yet: the problem was all the tough breaks he'd had in life. These came in many varieties, but Billy's tough breaks all had one thing in common: they generally pointed the finger at someone else. The culprits ranged from other companies and individuals, to family members, to God and His timing; it seemed like many people had done Billy wrong.

Now I had seen this symptom before, and I had learned that, when recited all together like Billy did, rarely are all those factors the primary problem. So I emphasized to Billy that strategic planning and business growth tactics are useless without the commitment to take full personal

---

1 The story combines several experiences with different people into one for illustrative purposes.

responsibility - and then to follow through. Own the plan, then do it, I told him. Allow God to direct you along the way, *but also believe Him to help you create an inspired plan to begin with – and then stick with His plan.*

Otherwise, I had learned, I would simply be wasting my time. When people are not willing to make a clear commitment up front, even someone like me who is knowledgeable and who really wants to help them can't do much. There is a wise saying: "I can stand *with* you, but I can't stand *for* you." This is so true. Years ago, while an associate pastor, I developed the following approach to people who came to me for counseling. Here's how I began many sessions: I told everyone who walked into my office that I was glad to help them, and glad they'd come. Then I'd go on to say that if - immediately following the session - they were not willing to put some things into practice I suggested, whether ideas they (1) 'thought they had tried', (2) 'didn't feel the need to try', or (3) 'hadn't considered yet' – then there was simply no need for us to meet! Our session would be over, and I would be glad to refer them to someone else.

After recovering from their initial shock, the couple would smile and nod in agreement. (I never had anyone walk out on me, but I saw a few consider it.)

Billy agreed that, though he had failed to follow through a few times before, this time he was ready to do things differently. And he seemed to mean it.

So with the help of a multi-disciplinary, seasoned team working closely with us, Billy and I came up with an inspired and tactically-sound plan, which all of us believed in. Billy raved that this was the most helpful experience he had ever been through. He was so excited to move forward, he could hardly wait to fly home and get to work.

But Billy's excitement barely outlasted his flight home.

We should have recognized trouble brewing when, just a few days later, we got the first call from Billy. Upon further reflection, he said, he had decided to pursue things in a different order; we needed to go back and revise the plan and provide him some different ideas, he told us.

We tried to remind Billy of his resolve to - for a season, at least - stick with the plan he'd already felt inspired to agree to.

But, citing some new idea he'd had, Billy threw out one of the most critical components of our plan to build his business without giving it a second thought or even realizing what he'd done. Later, after changing even more elements around and beginning to lose *any* coherent plan, his next phone calls switched to a familiar sound: the blame game. *Why hadn't we done this or that, and what about the other?* Suddenly, in Billy's mind, my team had become part of his life's problems, just like everybody else who had ever tried to help him.

I made the mistake of offering Billy some additional coaching, because I deeply desired to see him enter into His highest God–given potential. (For me, there is nothing like seeing a person fulfilling their Destiny; nothing. I *love* it. And his breakthrough was so close at hand, I could see it!) As we continued our conversations though, the ball never stayed with Billy. When things didn't go his way, everyone else was at fault.

Why did Billy revert back to the way he had always done things, despite his real desire to move forward? That's a good question. I don't know why, maybe he simply lacked the discipline to break his bad habits. Unfortunately, stories like Billy's are all too common. Years later, while many other people, projects, and plans have advanced, Billy, as far as I know, remains in the same spot, if not worse off: still blaming others and hoping that someone else will solve his problems for him. He still hasn't completely accepted his personal responsibility. Yet there is no doubt in my mind that Billy has seeds of greatness in him, just as you do. However, Billy's have not yet blossomed the way they could.

Perhaps you've had some failures in life yourself, David, and have wondered what went wrong. Hopefully you'll discover the answer as we continue spending time together.

Why Your Choices & Actions Matter

David, remember this: bridging the gap between where you are and where you believe God intends takes <u>responsibility</u> and <u>follow-through</u>, in addition to Faith.

Think about this for a minute. You have been given a life. You have been well made, handsomely gifted, and clearly called. You have been positioned in the right place, at the right time, for a purpose. You have been given an Internal Compass, an Inspired Guide Book, and a Supremely Able Helper. You have been encouraged to seek God.

You have not been *forced* to comply, to operate in God's grace, or to live according to His principles. He surely helps and rewards those who make right choices, but He does not *force* those decisions.

They are up to you.

Your choices and actions matter. You are responsible for them. Wherever you are, those choices and actions are a major reason you are there.

No one is going to do everything for you, or is entirely responsible for *your* choices, *including God.* You can do His will, of course. *But even that is a choice!* I can see you nodding your head like you already know this, but think deeper for a minute. Not your pastor, business partner(s), spouse, ministry leaders, sponsor, friends, parents, mentor, coach, fans, other associates, extended family, kids, or wealthy benefactors are responsible for the choices you make in life, David.

Reclaim your Destiny out of the hands of others and out of circumstances you can't control, and bring it back squarely between you and God.

Take responsibility for moving things in the right direction - through wise choices and actions - while simultaneously relying on God's help.

Bridging the gap between where you are and where you want to be takes responsibility and follow-through, in addition to Faith.

Believe Him for His game-changing grace and mercy every step of the way, but don't expect Him to do the tasks He's enabled you to do. *You* have to respond to the opportunities you are given in life. Ultimately, no one else is accountable.

Remember, David, this is a test. If it makes you feel somewhat uncomfortable or even momentarily discouraged, that is not uncommon.

The question is, can you press through anyway? The amazing truth is that you are designed to function best while embracing personal responsibility. I know it can seem troubling, but don't give up here: it's only a first test.

You need to take responsibility not only for your choices and actions in general, but also take specific responsibility to effectively manage and care for the people and projects you want to move forward – including any groups, businesses, departments, or organizations you are in charge of, or intend to create.

This doesn't mean that you don't trust or believe for the best from others. Of course you do that; you need them and they need you. And of course you count on God. After all, even when you falter, He weaves His influence into the fabric of your decisions and shares His grace to pull you toward your Destiny. But don't get caught in the trap of letting life just happen to you as you float along. God has invested more in you than that. Take the initiative to be a Change Agent rather than expecting others to do this for you, or *instead* of you.

You will never fulfill your God-given potential alone, but you can't get there without also taking personal responsibility!

Some people believe that God is the direct cause of everything that occurs in their lives. However, God is not the initiator of every human action or event - and I imagine He's tired of everyone thinking He is. When a teenager is brutally raped, a parent heartlessly drowns their child, or the consuming greed of one person steals hard-earned money from thousands, do you actually believe God initiated those events? No, and that goes for countless others circumstances as well.

God has given individual *people* the stunning right to make decisions and choose actions. While turning completely to Jesus removes the penalty for sin, and simultaneously opens the door to eternal life (AMAZING!), here is where many Christians get confused: *how a person chooses to invest their*

> *God is not the initiator of every human action or event - and I imagine He's tired of everyone thinking He is.*

27

life __as a Christian__ can yield additional reward – or none. (This is not to be confused with working one's way into heaven or trying to add to what Jesus has accomplished. That's a separate matter; a matter of one's individual choices and actions post-conversion.)

> "But on the judgment day, fire will reveal what kind of work each builder has done. The fire will show if a person's work has any value. If the work survives, that builder will receive a reward. But if the work is burned up, the builder will suffer great loss. The builder will be saved, but like someone barely escaping through a wall of flames."
>
> *1 Cor. 3:13-15 NLT*

David, I do not want you to be among those caught off guard by this. When some Christians stand before God, prepared to shift blame as if they weren't responsible for any decisions of their lives other than to accept Christ, a surprise is coming! They will be saved, an astonishing reward in itself, but most of their life's work will be completely lost.

However, the flipside is far more remarkable. The King of the Universe has planned special rewards for you, for choosing worthwhile targets to aim your life toward! And He's sent the Supremely Able Helper to assist you every step of the way. So how will you choose to invest your life here? That's the question. To His call *you* must respond; to the challenges of life *you* must step up.

Please make sure you pass this test, David. It's not fleshly, selfish, or unspiritual - it's essential. Go ahead and close this book for a while if you need to, but don't leave this point without embracing full responsibility for your decisions and actions as a Christian. Your choices affect this life and ring through eternity. Yes, of course God will forgive you for wrong ones - when you simply apologize properly, turn away from them, and ask Him to.

But all your decisions and actions form a direction. Make it the right one.

Let me say this one last way before we move on. Embracing this kind of personal responsibility is <u>not</u> God leaving you to your own devices, or forcing you to resign yourself to only what you can accomplish in your own strength. Absolutely not! Depend on God, while also doing all He has enabled *you* to do. Soon, you'll be working together with Him in a wonderful new way.

Good, David! Very, very good. You are one step closer to slaying a Giant.

Chapter 3

Key Takeaways & Giant Slayer Tips

- You **must not live passively**, simply hoping for things to change for the better. They probably won't.

- *Your* **choices and actions** make a profound difference in the trajectory of your life.

- To release the **full measure of grace** your life can deliver, continue along a path of wise decisions.

- **Bridging the gap** between where you are and where you believe God intends you to go takes <u>responsibility</u> and <u>follow through</u>, in addition to Faith.

- No one else is going to do everything for you, nor are they entirely **responsible for *your* choices**, *including God*.

- **Take initiative to be a Change Agent** rather than expecting others to do it.

Chapter 4
Searching for Destiny

"...anyone who belongs to Christ has become a new person. The old life is gone; a new life has begun!" *2 Cor. 5:17 NLT*

Don't those words thrill your heart? They get me every time. The moment you and I were born into the Kingdom, we began entirely new lives. What an amazing miracle: the old life gone and a brand new one in its place! Hooray!!!

Yet, just like me, David, you probably have days where you feel like your new life doesn't seem much different from the old one. I don't mean where you lose hope that you are going to heaven or anything like that. I mean times when your *here-and-now* seems frustratingly similar to what any average person is doing.

I'm sure you've wanted to know what's possible *right now in your new life that wasn't possible before.* After all, you are *here* now. Are dreams of making a real difference on planet Earth out of line? Absolutely not. The fact is you have an incredible Destiny, a story that God is writing through you, and with you. However, it's not just any old tale, and it takes wholehearted commitment to live it to the utmost.

Despite a host of readily available and well-written books about surging into Destiny, almost every day I meet people who have read many, but have yet to enter theirs. How very frustrating! Some of these people cope by giving up on 'Destiny' altogether, or by convincing themselves to settle for less. Others feel as if they once caught a glimpse of Destiny, but missed a particular opportunity and now can't go back. (At the time, perhaps they ended up choosing a more familiar, seemingly safer route.) Then there are those who remain poised to seize the opportunity as soon as they recognize it, ever eager to launch headlong into what only God could have prepared - and never look back.

How about you?

The Real Problem: Connecting the Dots

Here's a common problem. It seems that it's one thing to **discover** a passion, a purpose, or calling, but a whole different matter to bridge the gap to actually doing it! *How does one connect the dots?* That's the tricky part. To complicate matters, widespread 'how-to' advice only helps a fraction of the people searching for help. The advice frequently comes in the form of a one-size-fits-all solution, as if every person must have arrived miraculously at the same spot in life, and therefore a simple formula will get each one from point 'A' to point 'B'.

Before you dismiss all your dreams as worldly, impossible, or somehow ineligible – or bravely accept that just doing the best you can for now is all you should think about - I hope you'll allow yourself a another look.

Life is not that simple. Mine's not, and yours probably isn't either. Many Destiny-seekers struggle to find the lasting lift they need to soar into the wondrous, preferred future they dream of - even having in hand a 'Foolproof 7-Step Plan' they memorized.

The truth is, many of us wake up one day and question whether the life we are living is below what is truly possible with God. And if we decide it is, what then? We consider different reasons why a gap exists between *where we are*, and *where we feel destined to be*. Maybe it's insufficient finances, the press of parenting, lack of training or opportunity, relationships we need or lost, bad decisions, lack of experience or Faith, or past failure, or sickness, or tragedy, or...; the list goes on. Maybe we're too old, too young, too busy, or too tired. Perhaps fear or uncertainty holds us back, even if we don't call it that. Or maybe other Giants stand in the way.

In any event, David, whether you're presently discouraged and confused, or triumphant and expectant; whether you feel right on track with God or far away from Him - or any combination in between - any place you are right now is fine. However, as Destiny calls louder, and it will, expect to see new steps worth taking. Most people come to a day when they sincerely desire to move toward something greater, but find themselves trapped in present circumstances, wondering how to proceed - or if they even can. Maybe you are somewhere near that point?

If so, what should you do? While *studying* Destiny can produce invaluable moments of clarity, a resulting new-found *desire* to move forward more purposefully is not the same thing as hitting that mark. **The world is full of Christians who believe that more is possible with God, yet they aren't experiencing it. Why not?!** I run into them all the time and I'll bet you do too! For example, in a recent survey at one of my workshops, almost 4 out of 5 admitted that there was a rather large difference between what is actually happening in their lives versus what they believed God intends.

Why is there such a *Destiny Gap*? Can it be crossed? Should it be? Are our aspirations off-base? Are we simply missing the path of our own Destiny somewhere? For that matter, should we even allow ourselves to think so big?

David, before you dismiss all your dreams as worldly, impossible, or somehow ineligible – or bravely accept that just 'doing the best you can' for now is all you should think about – I hope you'll allow yourself another look. Destiny Thieves come in many forms, and some sound quite convincing. I don't want you to be tricked out of that greater future you were born for. I think you'll find that some of your deepest desires aren't as crazy as they might seem, even if others must be left behind.

And keep this in mind: your journey of Destiny doesn't have to look like what others think it should. It often won't. And why should it? After all, they are not its author. In some moments, your earnest pursuit will inevitably raise eyebrows. So what? The route is tricky in parts and often quite humbling. And even at the end, what is great to you may not appear that way to someone else. No matter; stay the course, my new friend! The rewards of digging deep to pursue your Destiny are truly great, so don't give in to the predictable chants of ordinary naysayers (of whom the world is full).

Where's Destiny Hiding?

Since many would agree that too few people experience the full measure of their God-given potential, the question is *why*. Aren't we designed by God Himself for Destiny, to serve the purpose He intends completely, and with exceptional effect? Shouldn't that path also lead to the words every Kingdom citizen wants to hear, "Well done, good and faithful servant!"

If so, why is that route sometimes so hard to find? Well, David, just knowing you have a divine purpose, an important mission here on Earth, is a place to start. But that's only the beginning. I recently heard this put another way: "So you're a Christian? Big deal. Now what?!" Paul recognized the importance of moving forward, and it urged him on:

> "Not that I have already attained, or am already perfected; but I press on, that I may lay hold of that for which Christ Jesus has also laid hold of me." *Phil. 3:12 NKJV*

Like the apostle Paul, Jesus laid hold of you because He loves you, David, and in His love there is also purpose.

Your True Identity & Special Assignment

God designed each one of us to make a difference: a particular difference. Just like Jesus and Paul, there is special work for each Kingdom citizen to do, *right here on Earth*. But some complete their mission, while others don't.

Here's what Jesus said about His mission:

> "I glorified you on earth by completing down to the last detail what you assigned me to do." *John 17:4 MSG*

Jesus had a Special Assignment, and so do you. Jesus didn't just do whatever He felt like, and then ask God to bless it. His Special Assignment came from God, and yours does too.

You also have a True Identity, which is yours alone from God. You are created in His image and are therefore unique. The Inspired Guidebook also tells us that 'as He was in this world so are we'. In this world Jesus was a distinct person, capable of individual thought and action, who ultimately overcame the world. As we follow Him we are to do the same.

What is crucial to know, David, is that seeking to learn your True Identity and fulfill your Special Assignment keeps you moving toward Destiny. Trying to be someone else or do something else (knowingly or not), only leads to disappointment, heartache, and trouble.

We'll look more into your True Identity and Special Assignment later, to help you clarify them.[2] But the purpose of this section is for you to see *how to hit the mark with your life, once you sense a basic heading.* For when you catch a glimpse of your true purpose, you eventually discover it is well beyond your individual ability, and also that formidable obstacles stand in your way. What then?

Knowing *what* to do is only part of the equation; here I want to talk to you about the other part: actually *doing* it.

(As we move along, you will likely gain additional insight regarding your True Identity and Special Assignment, so do **not** despair if you lack

---

2 The Giants Workbook offers additional discovery tools for those who would like to explore more about this.

focus in that department. Sometimes everyday life has a way of stifling the 'what' – the inkling from God - to such a degree that it seems entirely lost when it's really present, but it just seems crazy or unrealistic. Anyway, you likely have more of a clue than you think, and might actually be stuck more on the *how* than the *what*. But if you aren't sure about your True Identity or Special Assignment, that's okay for now.)

For the moment, and as an act of Faith, David, walk with me as if you already have *some* insight from the Lord about your True Identity and Special Assignment. This could be as general as wondering if your passion for music and your desire to help children may one day come together in a new way, or as specific as a detailed personal mission statement that you have been working toward for years. Whatever you have, bring it. Don't get bogged down here trying to get perfect clarity; keep moving and believing.

Remember, we walk by Faith.

Destiny Detours

Knowing now that you have at least *some* inspired direction, the question is: why would you ever allow yourself to get sidetracked from it? I mean, if you have a Special Assignment from God, why on earth would you ever let it go?

Well, this happens to many Kingdom citizens, unfortunately. And frequently, detours from the call of Destiny can be traced back to believing some kind of lie. For example, imagine a person who hears the lie that they are useless and worthless. They could come to believe this lie, and so eventually give up on life and hope. This would be a terrible tragedy, because of course the truth is exactly the opposite: every person is valuable, dearly loved and cherished by God.

And of course there are a lot of other messages out there contrary to what God tells us in the Inspired Guidebook, and contrary to what I'm telling you. We are all bombarded with these messages 24/7 and everywhere we turn, the same lies that those Giants tried to get me to believe at the city vision meeting: "You can't change anything important."

"You're nobody special." "Don't waste your time trying to fulfill your Destiny." "You can't stop us!"

You are Not a Nobody

By now you have hopefully learned to spot most of these lies. However, there is a certain type of lie which is especially toxic, because it comes from those among us, not those outside. Outsiders ridiculing us and our Faith shouldn't surprise us. But when harmful information comes from those we trust, it's harder to counter, because we may not realize it's even happening.

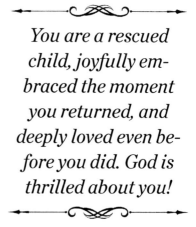

You are a rescued child, joyfully embraced the moment you returned, and deeply loved even before you did. God is thrilled about you!

What I'm talking about, David, is when well-meaning Christians put you down in ways that can sound truthful, but aren't. These Kingdom citizens make it sound as if God sees you as a nobody, by telling you continually how wretched you are through and through. That may have been true *before* you became a child of God, but it is no longer true now, because God has rescued you and made you new at the core, and it's an insult to what He suffered and accomplished to say otherwise. It's also destructive and limiting to your future.

Of course you aren't perfect; no one is. But continuing to beat yourself up – or allowing others to accuse you - with the way you used to be, keeps you enslaved by a Giant lie. Deep down, you are not that person anymore, David, but a wonderfully recreated person, now capable of great things. While apart from Him you can do nothing, you are no longer apart from Him, and you know that.

You are not a Nobody, you are a Somebody. *You are a rescued child, joyfully embraced the moment you returned, and deeply loved even before you did. God is thrilled about you!*

Can you see how believing a (truthful-sounding) lie can push you off course from Destiny?

Working to Earn God's Acceptance

Here's another example of a lie that brings a Destiny Detour: <u>the idea that you need to work *for* God's acceptance</u>. Now the truth is this:

> **"...according to the good pleasure of His will, to the praise of the glory of His grace, by which He made us accepted in the Beloved."**
> *Eph 1:5-6 NKJV*

You are already accepted by His grace! You can't work FOR His approval; you already have it. He made you accepted. You work FROM approval. That is a HUGE difference. Yes, you still work, but the motivation is completely different. *People who don't learn this difference waste untold amounts of their lives trying to climb up to a place where in reality they are actually already standing.* What a horrible, vicious burden!

Destiny Boosters

I want you to also be on the lookout for those things which help pull you along. There are obvious boosters, such as studying your Inspired Guidebook, keeping the right kind of company, and unashamedly worshipping God. Yet there are less obvious ones too. For example, a powerful Destiny boosting force is simply knowing that **God's remedy for your mistakes is far more powerful than the consequences of your actions!**

Imagine being in an accident and breaking your arm badly in several places. The doctors tell you that because of spreading infection, they'll likely have to amputate your arm. If the doctors instead managed to save your arm and it healed *just enough* so you could feel your fingers again, that would be great. If you were actually able to use your arm a little, that would be extraordinary. But what if your arm were miraculously healed better than it was to begin with, and you started throwing touchdown passes you couldn't throw before with your undamaged arm? That would be downright incredible!

But this is exactly what God's solutions to your mistakes are like, David. His solutions are so much greater than your original problem, you're better off than before! It's not 'just barely enough', it's more than enough!

"So does that mean I should mess up just to get the cure?"

No, it doesn't, but that's a story for another time and place! (There are preferred ways to experience God's provision.) Here is the point. There is a higher principle at work in your life now. *It's called the Law of the Spirit of Life.* It propels you toward Destiny, especially when you learn to tap into it by Faith. And as you do tap in, it begins to work 24 hours a day bringing *additional* good things to you, lifting you in the right direction - not simply counteracting negative consequences. Can you see the difference? I am telling you this because Destiny Boosters like these help you accomplish what is otherwise impossible.

You and I still make mistakes, despite our best efforts. But because of the work God has already completed on our behalf, even continued mistakes don't mean you are worthless or unqualified for additional blessings from Him. Fall down? Look up. Kneel down. Get up. Keep walking. …Fall down again? Look up. Kneel down. Get up, keep going, thanking God that His solution is greater than your problem. …Fall down again? Look up. Kneel down. Get up. Just keep moving.

It's truly that simple, David, because you're working *with* God now! You're part of the family, the team. He wants to lift you! Sincerely seek Him, and once you have done the best you can to understand His will – get moving in that direction! Of course you need to do your best to make sure you keep heading in the right direction - but don't second-guess every step; you'll never experience what God intends for you while thinking like that. The most exciting part is that God's plans for you fit the way He made you! So you'll find clues when you investigate how He did design you, by looking at such things as your passions, talents, personality, and unique circumstances.

As you move further toward the call of Destiny, David, you'll come to a point where you realize, deep down, that *what God has put in your heart to do is actually*...impossible. That's right, I said IMpossible. And I don't mean in just a theoretical way, either, or just so I can sound spiritual. I mean absolutely impossible in the practical, everyday sense of *not doable.*

I mean that what God has called you to do in life, David, you cannot

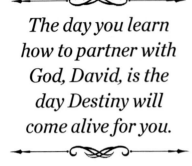

The day you learn how to partner with God, David, is the day Destiny will come alive for you.

achieve by your own efforts, no matter how clever and talented you are.

Now while many people come to see this truth, this unclimbable wall across the Road to Destiny, few make it past. Because there is only one way to get past this roadblock...and that way, my friend, is to *learn how to partner with God.*

One of Life's Greatest Opportunities

Let me ask you a question, David. To be God's Partner, I mean to really *work with Him* daily, wouldn't that be one of the most fulfilling things you could ever experience in life?

Can you imagine the joy of sharing your entire day together with the All-Powerful Creator, working purposefully with Him as if *you* belonged by *His* side? Laughing, sharing, and enjoying His sweet presence as you worked, you'd barely be able to stand the wonderful times you were having. And talk about results! There's no telling what you would accomplish with HIM as your partner.

Ah, but I can hear those Giants now:

"Really now, haven't you got the message that God doesn't need your help, and is doing you a favor to let you even exist? So why start getting big ideas about partnering with Him? It's far too dangerous to think like that. It's also crazy. Who knows, He might even zap you!"

Or maybe:

"Surely if a real partnership with God was even possible, it would be reserved for just a few full-time pastors, missionaries, and select super-spiritual individuals. And besides, God's not really interested in the kinds of things you are good at and like to do, anyway. The best thing to do is just get back to your normal life. Sure, it's boring sometimes, but it's not really <u>that</u> bad – and it's safe! And anyway, that must be the right thing

to do, since that's what most people do – all <u>normal</u> and intelligent people, at least!"

(A fine mess we're in now, thinking like this. Okay, it's clearly time to stop listening to Giants and those who sound like them!)

That may be what most people do, David, but most people have it wrong. This is one of the greatest secrets never told, that God not only loves you, forgives you, enjoys you, and wants to share eternity with you, but *He wants to be YOUR PARTNER* right here on planet Earth, right now!

The day you learn how to partner with God, David, is the day Destiny will come alive for you.

Chapter 4
Key Takeaways & Giant Slayer Tips

- You have an **incredible Destiny**, a story that God is writing through you, and with you.

- Jesus had a **Special Assignment** on Earth, and so do you.

- You also have a **True Identity**, which is yours alone from God. You are created in His image, and you are unique.

- You are a rescued child, joyfully embraced the moment you returned, and deeply loved even before you did. **God is thrilled about you.**

- You **cannot work FOR** God's approval; you already have it.

- God not only loves you, forgives you, enjoys you, and wants to share eternity with you; **He wants to be YOUR PARTNER.**

Chapter 5
When Going for God Falls Flat & 3 More Tough Roadblocks

"...take on an entirely new way of life — a God-fashioned life..."
Eph. 4:24 MSG

If it's possible to partner with God, how come more Christians don't? What's stopping us? What's stopping you? There are four major roadblocks that rob Kingdom citizens of this remarkable opportunity.

Roadblock #1: Doing Things FOR God Instead of WITH Him

When I first met my wife she was driving a car with the license plate "GO4GOD". (I didn't pay much attention to it, because the driver was so stunning! But eventually I noticed it.) That peppy little red car served her well as she zipped around town; it worked better than the license plate motto.

Here's what I mean. When you understand that God sent His Son to save you from yourself and give you a brand new life with Him, it's natural to feel so thankful that you want to try to find a way to pay Him back. It seems reasonable, and this is exactly what most people are taught. But the price is far beyond what you and I - or anyone for that matter - could ever hope to pay. So this noble idea, rather than helping us, falls flat. It can seriously damage your ability to Partner with God, even though the motive is good.

It's not wrong to want to do things FOR God. In fact, all Christians do. Anyone who has met God and given their life to Him wants to please Him. Don't you? Of course! Even in the smaller parts of everyday life, when someone does nice things for you, the natural response is to do good to them in return.

Going *for* Him, in the sense of pursuing Him is fantastic; by all means seek Him with your whole heart! On the other hand, going for Him, as in trying to fulfill your Special Assignment *for* Him, gets you worn out and way off track.

So instead, you must be utterly determined do things WITH God, rather than FOR Him, David.

Commit yourself to this completely. As God's partner, you can't let yourself drift toward thinking that your Special Assignment is like homework: the teacher gives it to you, you do it on your own, and then bring it back for a grade. Not only does that not get your Assignment done, it also limits the flow of His help in doing what you have been called to do. Double whammy. Working for God wears you out because you are incapable of fulfilling your Destiny without His help.

> *You must be utterly determined do things WITH God, rather than FOR Him.*

But even knowing this, it's easy to fall back into working alone. After all, before you met God, that was all you knew how to do. So when you find yourself struggling in human strength by itself, apologize to your Partner, reconfirm your commitment to working together, and make a point to invite Him into your activities.

Communicate with Him as you work. This takes time and practice, but your Partner is patient and kind.

David, listen closely. The way to Partner with God is narrow. To defeat Goliaths and accomplish great things in the everyday world, you and I must change. God loves all His children, but Partnership He reserves for mature sons and daughters. Many sincere, gifted believers know *about* this truth, but they choose not to put it into practice.

It does take commitment. But you can do it, David. You are different.

Roadblock #2: Not Knowing Partnership is Even an Option

That's a great start, determining to move forward *with* God instead of *for* Him. You passed the first roadblock, David, but here is the second obstacle. You know that God has promised He will never leave you or forsake you. So He is always right there with you, whether or not you are doing right or wrong.

"So *what's the big deal about Partnering if He is always with me wherever I go anyway*?"

Great question; here's the thing: **Just because you have become a Kingdom citizen, joined the family, and the Supremely Able Helper is in you, does not mean that you are operating as a partner.**

"*Really?*"

Yes. You can be in God's Kingdom, one of His children, but not working as His partner.

The Generous Man & the Eager Orphan

Imagine a generous man who is also a highly successful entrepreneur. This man adopts an orphan. The orphan, now his legal daughter, thrives in her new home and grows to love her new dad. As the years pass, they become closer and closer. They share all kinds of fun times together. She begins to help out in the family business doing small jobs here and there; it's so much fun to work with Dad!

Eventually, the daughter takes a full-time position in one of her father's companies, and then is promoted to manager. After a few years, she wants to start her own new business. She talks to her dad about it and he likes the idea.

A smart woman and quite capable, in the beginning she holds her own. But it's a lot of work, and soon she finds herself short on money, expertise, and time. So she grits her teeth and doubles her efforts. She starts taking fewer breaks and working later. She wants to succeed and show everyone, especially her dad, that she can do it. Reaching out to some friends and smart business people for input, she studies every book she can get her hands on. Things improve some, but only temporarily.

Finally, she decides that she'd better get a partner before it's too late, or else the company won't survive. She needs an excellent counterpart who can contribute in multiple ways. She puts the word out and starts looking. Finally she finds someone who seems like a perfect fit and signs him up. Unfortunately, after a short while it's clear that the new partner will be unable to gather the money he said he could, or to fulfill all the other promises he made. Eventually, despite a valiant effort, the business goes under.

The daughter is heartbroken, worn out, and embarrassed. She meets her dad for coffee one day and he comforts her. "Dad," she says, "I just don't know what I could have done differently. Among other things, I definitely chose the wrong partner." Jokingly, she adds, "I wish I could have teamed up with someone powerful and wise like you, Dad."

"Why didn't you ask me?" he replies, looking puzzled.

"Ask YOU, to be my partner? Oh, Dad, you have too many other more important things to do. I knew you wouldn't want to help me with my little idea. It's not even the business you are in."

"Sweetheart, I would have jumped at the opportunity to partner with you," he responded. "All you had to do was ask. I would have given you the money and expertise you needed, and many other resources also. Why don't we work together on your next project?"

It's tragic that so many people never see the possibility of Partnering with God, and so they waste one of life's greatest opportunities.

That deep desire for meaningful accomplishment you have, David, that longing to dream big, is there because God put it in you. It's not wrong to want to accomplish great things. The way some Christians order their lives you would think that anyone with dreams and goals is selfish. While some aspirations are off-base, not all are. Those are the ones you need to explore further: the God-Kind.

But just because someone is a Christian doesn't mean they know anything about Partnering with God. Why do so many people miss out? Think about a marriage for a moment and it may become clear. Wives and husbands are *lovers*. Ideally they are also *friends*. If they have children, they become *parents*. A wife and husband could go on the hit TV series *Amazing Race* and be *teammates,* or start a business and become *co-founders*. They could have a mortgage together and be *co-signors*. If one got sick the other might become a *caregiver*. One or both are *providers*. The list goes on. There are many different roles and dimensions to their relationship, yet they are still only two people.

If you think about partnership for a second, David, it is a different type of relationship than being a family member or a friend. Because the orphan had been adopted and had spent time with her father, their relationship grew. It was fulfilling to both of them. But what she attempted with her life, the dream she wanted to accomplish, never became what it could without his involvement.

Partners *accomplish things together*. They don't simply spend time with each other; they work together toward shared goals. And a true Partnership is not an off-again, on-again arrangement where you come and go whenever you feel like it – it's a *sustained collaboration*.

Why else would you form a Partnership? That law firm down the street was formed because effective partnerships accomplish great things. What I'm saying is that your relationship with God is also like this. He can be Lord, Father, Almighty, Friend, Counselor, Savior, Ruler, Teacher, Deliverer and so on, and you can be son, servant, friend, lover, worshiper and more - yet never *partner*. Partnering takes nothing away from any of these aspects, any more than two people getting married means they can no longer be friends. What amazing fulfillment is missed when lovers aren't also friends! And what a terrible loss when Christians don't learn to Partner with God.

I can tell you see what I mean. If you never learn how to Partner with God, David, you will always have a feeling deep down inside you that there should be more to life.

If you can accomplish what's in your heart in the everyday world without Partnering with God, your goal is too small. Even worse, doing _anything_ without Him is doing it wrong.

Roadblock#3: Failing to Understand Your True Identity

The Obstacle in the Mirror

> "So you are no longer a slave, but God's child: and since you are his child, God has made you also an heir." _Gal. 4:7 NIV_

Well, we've explored doing things WITH God, David, and a couple of things that get in the way of partnering with Him. By getting past the first two roadblocks, you might think you have almost arrived. After all, those were important obstacles to clear. But unfortunately, even though you have made it a long way, we have to go further still. In fact, this next challenge is a bit more difficult than the first ones. Just know this: beyond this challenge is a reward so great that it makes this next fight well worth it. I kid you not.

Yet this is the battle most people never win.

But David, if you read closely and listen with your heart, you can conquer this one, too. As you do, your potential to enter partnership with God will skyrocket, and you'll move closer to the life you have imagined deep in your heart. And that's no small matter.

Now please listen closely. **_What is most likely to stop you from entering your partnership with God - and therefore limit your future - is what_** *you believe about the person staring back at you in the mirror.*

No - it's not Giants or God or circumstances. Look in the mirror, David. Who do you see? What's that person capable of? How do you feel about the life of that person? Pleased? Disappointed? Hurt? Angry? Blessed? Frustrated? Loved? Indifferent? Ashamed? Tired? Hopeful? Look at yourself for a minute: you're not completely sure, are you? Maybe you have mixed feelings. That's fine; be honest.

Now here's what I want you to do next.

I want you to face the fact that some things you currently believe about yourself are completely wrong, and that those false beliefs are no accident. Not <u>possibly</u>, but <u>definitely</u>. You have adopted some wrong beliefs about yourself; everyone has.

But which ones are wrong? Not everything you think is wrong, of course; but anything you believe about yourself that is not part of your True Identity is wrong, and these false beliefs will keep you from effectively partnering with God.

What do I mean by your True Identity?

Your True Identity is the one God alone has given you. Do you remember Gideon, from the Inspired Guidebook? His tale contains great truths about the power of True Identity. If you'll allow them to, I believe these truths can change your life right now.

Two Great Secrets of Gideon's Success

Gideon's was a time when God's people did mostly evil in His sight. So to teach them a lesson, God handed them over to their enemies for seven years. Those enemies were cruel and numerous, and God's people were sometimes forced to hide out in caves to escape being killed. Their enemies stole all the livestock and even attacked the crops, so nothing would grow. Starvation set in.

Then, only then, did His people begin to cry out to God for help.

Gideon was threshing grain that he had somehow managed to save, hiding inside a large stone winepress to do it. Can you picture that poor guy, trying to work while terrified every moment that his life would be snuffed out by the enemy who prowled daily? How would you like to be working a job where you could literally lose your life at any minute? Talk about being backed into a corner! Not a great spot to find yourself in. Gideon had lost practically everything and had to hide just to survive. That's sure a lot worse off than most people I know today.

But then God sent an angel to Gideon, with a bizarre and wonderful message:

> "Mighty hero, the Lord is with you! ...Go with the strength you have, and rescue Israel from the Midianites. I am sending you!" *NLT Judg. 6:12 & 14*

Gideon probably thought to himself. "Huh? What? Yeah, right. Uh, Lord, apparently You don't see what's happening here. Have you lost touch with reality?" Then Gideon goes on to remind the Lord who he really was by saying:

> "But Lord," Gideon replied, "how can I rescue Israel? My clan is the weakest in the whole tribe of Manasseh, and I am the least in my entire family!" *NLT Judg. 6:15*

Gideon reminded God that he was the weakest of the weak, the most unqualified person around. That's how he saw himself anyway. Surely God must have made a mistake, thought Gideon.

But God did not agree!

God called Gideon *"Mighty Hero"*. That was Gideon's True Identity, despite all his limiting circumstances and contrary human opinions.

Most people answer to identities God did not give them, and they fail to answer to the one He did.

But Gideon remained unconvinced about his True Identity even though an angel brought the message! He kept questioning God. (You can read the whole story in your Inspired Guidebook: Judges 6-8.) Gradually though, Gideon came to see himself God's way, and when he embraced his *True Identity*, David, it made all the difference - just as it will for you. Gideon went on to deliver God's people and win some of the most famous battles of all time.

Most people don't realize that their True Identity is not just something worth knowing, it affects the outcome of their entire life. But had Gideon not come to believe God's perspective about him, he would never have made the amazing accomplishments that he did.

> *Most people answer to identities God did not give them, and they fail to answer to the one He did.*

How is that possible, to go from being the least of the bunch to suddenly being a great hero? Simply learning and embracing your True Identity is an incredible release point.

So what exactly is your *True Identity* and *how do you discover it?* Yes, you must get to the bottom of that, David. Your True Identity is not determined by the circumstances you find yourself in, how you see yourself, or even how others judge you by typical human measures. Your True Identity is how <u>God</u> sees you. He gave you your identity, and *He alone holds the key to it.*

The only way to grasp your True Identity is from Him: (1) paying attention to what He says about you in The Inspired Guidebook, (2) listening to what He whispers to your heart, and (3) embracing heavenly insights about you that He provides to others.

A Vicious, Calculated Attack

Let this sink in: <u>Your True Identity is, and has been, under attack</u>. It's vital to be aware of this.

You see, David, God's enemies know that if you discover who you truly are and what you are capable of in Partnership with God, some of the territories they have held for centuries are at risk. They would much prefer that you <u>never</u> discover the truth about your remarkable Giant-slaying potential. As far as they are concerned, the less you know about your True Identity and Special Assignment, the better. So they work ruthlessly in the everyday world to conceal these from you.

Giants are terrified of you entering into Partnership with God!

Learning how God sees the person in the mirror, despite all thoughts and evidence to the contrary: that's the solution. As long as you don't know your True Identity, you limit yourself and cannot be an effective partner. The biggest problem then is not outside - it's inside! Look at an example of how our own wrong beliefs can limit us:

> "...I can't tell you how much I long for you to enter this wide-open, spacious life. We didn't fence you in. The smallness you feel comes from within you. Your lives aren't small, but you're living them in a small way. I'm speaking as plainly as I can and with great affection. Open up your lives. Live openly and expansively!" *2 Cor. 6:11-13 MSG*

Look at this picture Paul paints for the Corinthians: people limiting themselves, living small lives - because of smallness from *inside!* No one else to blame. No fence actually there, but something *inside* stopping them. Holding wrong beliefs is like building fences inside you; a lack of awareness about your True Identity is like a prison.

David, you are supposed to be living a wide open, spacious life, and don't let anyone tell you different. Take the self-imposed limits off your life!

Now I have another important message for you: <u>God not only wants to be your partner, He genuinely likes working with you.</u> Do you hear me? I mean He really does: David, God likes working with you! Once I found out that God actually likes working with me in the everyday world - I mean genuinely enjoys it - my life has never, ever been the same. You can hear this truth from others all day long, but when you know it on the inside, it changes you.

For me, life is totally different than it used to be. God and I do everything together, and we enjoy each other.

An Amazing Ingredient and Mr. Zero

But there's even more. I'm sure you know that the most effective partnerships include *mutual respect.* David, I'm sure you respect God. But do you know that **God not only loves you and enjoys teaming up**

with you - *God <u>respects you</u> as His partner?* It's true; He said so Himself: "He who honors me, I will honor."

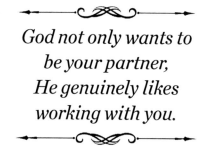

God not only wants to be your partner, He genuinely likes working with you.

I know you might have trouble with this idea at first; that's okay. But God is the one who has said it, so - especially since we respect Him above all others - we do need to forget what some people say, and instead believe Him: you, David, are an important part of this partnership. Sure, you've been told that God can do it all without you, and I'm sure He could. *But what you probably haven't been told as clearly is that He doesn't want to!* He wants to be your partner.

Take the book you hold in your hand, for example. Could God have written this, or a much better one, all by Himself? No question about that! But how *did* it come into being and appear in front of you? I certainly didn't try to do it all by myself. I intentionally partnered with God because that's what He led me to do; many of the secrets in here I hadn't a clue about until He helped me see them. I did not want to rely on my own little world and talents and wisdom by themselves to form this message and get in your hands: no way!

But on the flip side, I am not going to be one of those people who has the nerve to say: "Folks, it was all God, and Mr. Zero here, a real Nobody's Nobody, did absolutely nothing. So now if you and the other Humility Judges would please declare me humble..."

Think about this, David. Some people have the idea that "*all of Him and none of me*" is the way God wants it; they say that's humility, right? Well you know what? God had plenty of time to experiment with "all of Him and none of you" before He ever created you. Don't you think?!

Seriously, He had none of you before; why would He want to go back to that? He obviously doesn't, because He chose to create you. *He loves being with you and working together with you*, David, and you acknowledging this fact and choosing to Partner with Him honors Him. (And <u>not</u> acknowledging it actually dishonors Him.) Sure, He's the

Unbelievably Senior Partner, but by His amazing grace you, "little ole you", have made Partner in the family firm, my friend.

Think back to the Garden of Eden. Remember what happened after God created the animals?

> "Now the Lord God had formed out of the ground all the wild animals and all the birds in the sky. He brought them to the man to see what he would name them; and whatever the man called each living creature, that was its name." *Gen. 2:19 NIV*

God asked Adam to name the animals. Why didn't God handle that job all by Himself? He certainly didn't <u>need</u> Adam. David, are you seeing this? They did this *together.* Sure, the hardest part was creating the animals! But God is hardly insecure about His sons and daughters joining Him in creative accomplishment and playing a part; in fact, He enjoys it. The invitation to join Him, to Partner with Him, comes from Him!

Have you ever gone up to someone after they played a special piece of music at a Base Camp meeting and said, "Great job; your song was beautiful and it so encouraged me. Thank you for sharing your gift."

And then they responded with something spiritual sounding like "Oh, it was all God."

Excuse me, Madame Musician. I'm sorry to burst your bubble and I don't mean to be rude, but no, it wasn't all God: you actually practiced and then you actually sang. I saw you move your lips, and I know you rehearsed several times because the sound guy mentioned it. We give God the glory for the overall outcome and effect, but it was not 'all Him'. You two worked together, and it was a joy to experience, beautiful to see.

The skills and talents God has given you, David, are unique: you mustn't be afraid to sharpen them and to feel good about using them with Him; they are valuable in your Partnership. So don't fall for viewing your new self as less than God created you, just because some misguided people can't tell the difference between humility and disrespecting God's creation.

For you to get as far down the Road of Destiny as God wants you to, David, you need to think much differently about the only person who can truly limit your partnership with God: that obstacle in the mirror – YOU! You need to learn to see yourself as your heavenly Father sees you. *Since God respects you as His partner, you need to learn to respect yourself and your role in the partnership.*

Roadblock #4: Missing Your Special Assignment

"For we are His workmanship, created in Christ Jesus for good works, which God prepared beforehand that we should walk in them." *Eph. 2:10 NKJV*

David, think again about Roadblock #3, and what the angel told Gideon. "Mighty Hero" was Gideon's **True Identity**, and rescuing Israel from the Midianites was his **Special Assignment.** Knowing both his True Identity and his Special Assignment was crucial for Gideon, and it will be for you.

What then should *you* aim for? What are *you* supposed to be doing? Where can you make the greatest difference? How will you discover more about *your* Special Assignment? As someone has said, "If you're called to scale a mountain, make sure it's the right one before you start climbing." If you are going to Partner with God, you need to get a handle on this. But how?

As with True Identity, please remember that reaching this goal is NOT a microwavable self-discovery process. (I wish life were that simple!) Neither you nor I can force God to reveal something so extremely precious until you are truly ready - or before He is. Maybe your time is now - maybe it's in the future. However, what is possible is to help you see the value of knowing your Special Assignment, encourage you to expect God to reveal more as you walk with Him, and help you shed counterfeit assignments that may have attached themselves to you. The good news is that sometimes simply mulling over these matters can itself attract the aid of the Supremely Able Helper, and lead to moments of remarkable discovery.

Wearing the Wrong Suit

First, let's tackle a powerful lie head on. **Don't think for a minute that you can do whatever you set your mind to. You cannot and should not try that.**

"Huh? That doesn't sound very encouraging. What do you mean by that?"

This is the final great roadblock to partnership. Unfortunately, many parents, particularly here in the West, have been duped into telling their children that they can be anything they want to be. And most people have a hard time shedding things they were told repeatedly and early in life. Parents mean it as a way of opening up possibilities in the world, which of course is something any good parent tries to do. (Whether or not your parents told you this, the idea is probably lodged somewhere in your thinking from one of its many other sources, so we need to get rid of it.)

The problem is that you are not <u>designed</u> to do *anything* you happen to choose. Seriously; you're just not.

When something breaks down around our house, no one has ever accused me of being a mechanical genius or particularly good with my hands. Before I save a buck buying a piece of furniture marked '*some assembly required*', I think twice, maybe more. I'm not embarrassed about it and I don't use excess energy trying to make this obvious weakness my strength. I manage my weakness and take care of what requires my attention, but I don't rush to sign up for every chance to become a master carpenter.

Let's take this a step further. What if my Grandfather was a great mechanic, and I wanted more than anything to follow in his footsteps, so that I often dreamed of becoming like him? What if my mom and dad told me he was a great man, amazing with his hands, and they thought I could be like him - that 'all I had to do was set my mind to it.' What if I then trusted God to help me every step of the way, and I asked Him to Partner with me in my great plan?

So what's the problem? Well, being a mechanic has nothing to do with *my* Special Assignment; my Special Assignment involves working with people pursuing Destiny, not working with my hands. Would God still love me and be with me if I became a mechanic? Yes. Would I still be His son? Absolutely. Would my impact be nearly as great as if I went after *my* Special Assignment? No way; I'd be living life wondering why I had the funny feeling that so much more was possible.

"How can I be sure you're right about this?"

Because God creates things on purpose, not by accident. Therefore, since God created you, you have a special purpose, David. Your purpose is not the same as *anyone* else's. How can He make every person so unique? It boggles my mind, but He does.

You have a Special Assignment straight from the King; it's extremely unwise to invent a different one from scratch.

However, *inside* that area of Assignment lies plenty of fertile ground for inspired dreams to grow. Your Assignment isn't designed to restrict you - but to catapult you into your Destiny!

Learn More about <u>Your</u> Special Assignment

When you look at the unique combination of talents God has given *you* and the desires He has put in *your* heart, David, you find clues to discovering what you can best work on together. (One clue for me is that I'm not naturally skilled with tools.) *The wonderful thing is, your Special Assignment often includes things you already love to do and are good at.*

You don't think God cares about the knack He gave you for managing people in the business world, and so you should instead become a church pastor to please Him? You don't believe He likes football, enjoys seeing you use the special talent He gave you, and will partner with you every step of the way to becoming a pro? You can't imagine that your artistic talent, or love for architecture, or desire to help special needs kids, or aspiration to run for public office, or talent to make cool widgets or software or medical breakthroughs, or become a screenwriter, musician, or actress would EVER be something that could interest God in partnering with you?

Well, you're not the only one, I know. But how did we get to thinking like this?

There are billions of people on the planet, but only one you, David. If everyone did the exact same thing in the exact same way, how would such a monotonous world display the joyful, stupendous, unlimited creativity of a mind-bogglingly brilliant artist like God?

Of course it wouldn't.

Instead of hiding our individual lights, we should reflect His, and shine at our full brilliance right out in the everyday world so that others will be drawn to Him. Yes, we are all supposed to be agents of God's grace to a hurting world, but not everyone is designed to deliver God's grace *in the same form*. What will lead some people to God is not an evangelist, but the job that your business creates that helps them provide for their family, and the way you treat your employees.

If everyone tried to lead others to God like a traditional evangelist does, or if everyone took a vow of poverty, who would do everything else required to reach others and steward God's wonderful creation? Who would manage the outreach? Who would get to the places evangelists never go? Who would pay for plane tickets? Who would fly the plane?

Who would create great works of art that lift the spirit? Who would write books that thrill the heart and reveal God's love? Who would clean the buildings or make the sandwiches? Who would teach the children? Who would lead the city or enforce the law? Who would farm the crops, dance the jigs, build homes, or help educate people? Who would solve the problems of our day?

Who would negotiate terms on that new deal, invent the next amazing product, or sip coffee at the corner cafe while telling the story of how God rescued them? Who would send money to the relief efforts when disaster strikes, so that practical needs can be met? Who would create the TV series that draws people to God by the thousands? Who would act in the series or write the music?

Who would do all the wonderful things God has made possible as part of life, that when undertaken as His Partner become so much more?

You see what I'm talking about? And because you are unique, David, some of these tasks fit you - and many don't.

3 Common Pitfalls to Completing Your Special Assignment

Here are three pitfalls that commonly lead to a missed Special Assignment; one of them could be stopping you right now.

1. Trying to fit what someone else thinks you should do.
2. Doing your Special Assignment, but going about it in a way that doesn't fit you.
3. Trying to do someone else's Special Assignment.

None of these choices point you in the right direction, David; they are all like a suit that doesn't fit. If you aren't *supposed* to be like your Dad or your personal hero 'Kristina', trying to be like them is a waste of your precious life. Avoid moving either in a *direction* <u>or</u> *manner* that doesn't really fit you.

What comes as a result of knowing both your True Identity and your Special Assignment is simply irreplaceable! So don't settle for less.

Many opposing forces will try to get you off this course - don't follow them! You have to resist being pressed into a suit that does not fit; you must <u>break that mold before it breaks you!</u> You have got to be you: the real *you that God designed you to be.* The pressure to fit in, to not break tradition, and to do things in only one humanly-prescribed way will crush your spirit and rob you of the abundant life that God intended you to have.

But if you'll stand your ground, David, really being yourself, amazing things will begin to happen.

The suit that doesn't fit, and that limits your Partnership, is when you pursue anything other than your Special Assignment. The only way you'll ever reach your divine potential is in Partnership with God, moving in the direction He has called you.

So what is God sending you to do, David? Do you know? If not, ask Him; the answer to that question is your *Special Assignment*.

You're seeing the importance of this, David, I know you are. As you seek God to learn more about your True Identity and Special Assignment, a once in a lifetime opportunity comes about. This occasion is so powerful I can hardly wait share it with you. Please pay close attention and listen with your heart as we explore what happens.

Chapter 5

Key Takeaways & Giant Slayer Tips

- ☑ *Roadblock #1: Doing Things FOR God Instead of WITH Him.* You must be **utterly determined** do things WITH God, rather than FOR Him.

- ☑ *Roadblock #2: Not Knowing that Partnership is even an Option.* You can be in God's Kingdom, one of His kids, but not operating **as His Partner**.

- ☑ *Roadblock#3: Failing to Understand Your True Identity.* What's most likely to stop you from **entering your Partnership** with God - and therefore to limit your future - is what you believe about yourself. So believe what God says about you.

- ☑ *Roadblock #4: Missing Your Special Assignment.* You have a Special Assignment **straight from the King**. It's unwise to invent one from scratch. Seek God to discover more.

- ☑ True Partnership is not an off-again, on-again arrangement where you come and go whenever you feel like it – **it's a *sustained collaboration***.

"Help, I Still Don't Know What to Do!"

For those of you who might feel stuck about your True Identity or Special Assignment, here is a useful tip. In a recent Destiny workshop one participant raised a hand and exclaimed. "I still don't get it. I have no idea what I'm supposed to do." My wife then got up and said she felt an inspiration from the Lord. The message was simply this: *'stay by the line'*. As she explained it, I was reminded of a time when I hadn't a clue about anything God wanted me to do. None. The only thing I could think was that I had a passion for music. I remembered a few times many years before where I had felt special inspiration when playing and singing. That was it! *The funny thing is that I had given up music completely.*

Yet I wondered if some part of my Destiny could have something to do with music. So when a need arose in my local Base Camp for help in the sound booth, I showed up. When the worship team needed a sax player, I dusted mine off. When one of the prayer ministries needed some background music at 6am, I started playing keyboard again. When the youth group needed someone to lead worship, I gave it a try. I stayed by the only 'line' I could think of. Anyway, one thing led to another and eventually, staying by that line opened up the opportunity to become a full time Pastor in a fantastic local Base Camp. *Do not discount small beginnings or subtle inklings.* Find a way to participate somehow - if even in a small way - in the realm you believe you may be called to, and you may be surprised by what results.

Chapter 6
An Epic Intersection

"At every crossroads on the path that leads to the future, tradition has placed 10,000 men to guard the past." *Maurice Maeterlinck, Dramatist (1862-1949)*

David, if I told you there was a special entrance made just for you, where you could step into a more rewarding life – what would you think? I know, it sounds too good to be true, and maybe a little weird. A hidden door? What kind of nonsense is this?

That's okay, I know it might sound a little strange; but *what if* it is real? And if you could find this entrance and enter in, your life would become more like you've always hoped it would? I'm about to tell you about a place like that and how to find it. Then you be the judge. After all, I did say this book holds "keys" for Giant Slayers. *This one you won't want to miss.*

Many search their entire lives without finding the entrance I'm speaking of.

They don't find this place because they look where they *think* it should be, or might be, but it's not. Some give up; others keep wandering. But you can discover the entrance when you learn the secret. Pull up a chair and I'll tell you more.

I'm going to ask the Supremely Able Helper to make this come alive to you. You see, without His assistance, even when I tell you the location of this Great Entrance you wouldn't be able to see it. (It was the same way for me.)

I know this sounds like a mystery, but it's the truth.

The Great Entrance to Destiny

You already know that the most important door you could ever walk through is the one you entered when you believed in Jesus, the Son of God, and accepted the forgiveness He bought you with His life. There is no other door like that. But as central as it is, it's not the one I'm talking about. I'll tell you this, though. If you haven't yet walked through *that* door, you'll <u>never</u> find *this* one.

To help you locate this place, it helps to see God in a different way. You may not know this, David, but He's filled with surprises. (We'll discover more about that soon.) One of them is that He created a Great Entrance to Destiny for you. It's not a physical place, it's a spiritual one - but quite real. From what I can tell, this kind of door is especially useful for those living on the earth right now. You're here reading this book, *so you still have a chance to walk through yours.* Don't let the opportunity slip by.

Even those who find the way to Him often miss this place. The irony is that He wants you to find it, though few ever do. You can usually identify the ones who haven't found it, because they always feel like their lives were supposed to be more, but they just can't figure out what they've missed. Many of them lead solid, fruitful lives anyway. If only they could have learned this secret!

Let me share more. David, as we first spoke about your True Identity & Special Assignment, there was something I didn't tell you. *You see, even looking into these matters is a journey in itself.* Deeper discovery about your True Identity leads you along a road with God; greater

understanding of your Special Assignment is the same way. These roads are full of unexpected turns and hold many wonderful discoveries. Spiritually speaking they are literal pathways! (Remember, though your natural eyes rarely see them, spiritual things have substance. God Himself is a Spirit.)

Here's the secret you are looking for: *There is a place where these two roads come together.*

Let that idea fill your heart for a moment. Imagine the roads of your True Identity and Special Assignment winding through life, until, in one amazing moment: Pow!! They come together and suddenly you see it: *the Great Entrance to Your Destiny.* It's right at this divine intersection.

If you'll close your eyes and open your heart for a moment, you might even catch a glimpse of the door. It's incredibly large and beautiful, many times the size of any you are used to seeing. It won't look brand new because God has been working on it a long time for you.

And David, what is on the other side is even more breathtaking. I can't tell you all that's there because *you* must discover it for yourself, but I'll tell you this. Once you step through, an Unmistakable Imprint will appear in your life. Others will notice, and you will know it inside. The story of your life will become more compelling than ever before, and will point to Him more clearly.

Don't worry if you haven't gotten to your Great Entrance yet. It's nothing to be anxious about. You will get there by continuing to walk down both paths, so keep going.

And remember this: when your Great Entrance appears in front of you, you mustn't hesitate, but step right through. You see, some people get all the way to the entrance but, sadly, choose not to go through it. They think it's too big, or that it's meant for someone else. But it's for you.

The Unmistakable Imprint

Let me ask you a question. *Is there an Unmistakable Imprint of God on your life, David?* I don't just mean theologically, because He made you. I'm talking about an imprint that others can see: an observable demonstration of God's handiwork. Let's think about it like this. If a complete stranger came to live with you for an extended period, would that person be touched by Heaven? Would he or she recognize that God is *with you,* and would they then desire to know Him? To what degree? Would you have to work at it, or would it just happen?

I'm not asking whether you would take that person to Base Camp, study the Inspired Guidebook, engage in spiritual discussions, or avoid certain activities. Neither do I mean would you pray eloquently, share Truth passionately, or even serve commendably? Those are all good. But how *is* your sermon-without-words coming along - overall? Easy; don't be alarmed. No need to be defensive or justify yourself. I'm simply trying to help you see if you've found the Entrance yet. (Because it's a spiritual place, it is possible – although unlikely - to pass through and not know it.)

I'm asking how you *feel* about the progress of God's work in your life and the effect it is having on others. I know there are moments of His working in your life that are so unmistakable, they leave others feeling touched by Heaven. Wouldn't you like more moments like those? I sure would.

You don't have to be winning great masses to the Lord or shutting mouths of lions daily. But shouldn't there be an obvious connection between God being in your corner and what happens in your life every day? Aren't His power and love so amazingly great that they deserve to be seen through you to a degree that wins an exceptional harvest? Of course they are.

But few Kingdom citizens carry this kind of Heavenly imprint. Why not? Because they haven't found the place I'm telling you about, David.

Yet becoming a more powerful witness is just *part* of what happens once you go through the Great Entrance to Destiny. *When you pass through the Great Entrance to Destiny, your Partnership with God deepens and accelerates.*

Cruising Along the Road of Destiny

Partnership with God, your True Identity, and your Special Assignment are *all* crucial elements in the story God is writing with you. They are like three dancers leaping and moving in collective rhythm, able to create a far more beautiful and compelling scene together than if any danced alone. (Soon, you will also see that these three elements are essential in defeating Giants.) They work together to keep you moving along the Road of Destiny. In a very real way, walking in Partnership with God *is* Destiny.

Here is something else to keep in mind as you try to make sense of this. **Others will never be influenced by God through your life the way they could be if you are parked, out of harm's way, on the sidelines of your Special Assignment.** Your Special Assignment does look unsafe at times; no question about that. But when you wholeheartedly seek to accomplish the work God has created you to do instead of pursuing other things, you'll be especially well-cared for - despite the apparent danger.

When you achieve objectives along The Road of Destiny: i.e., meet needs, create value, give answers, slay Giants – right out in the everyday world where people can see it - your life will deliver truly abundant Grace. That kind of living is an unmistakable demonstration of God's loving, purposeful design for you. Walk through the Great Entrance and you'll see what I mean.

Ah well, David! Unless what I'm sharing gets all the way down in your heart, it's useless talk. So we can't stop quite yet. We must go deeper. But I think I've found a way…

Evidence of an Unmistakable Imprint

There is a special phrase in the Inspired Guidebook you need to learn. It harnesses the idea of *partnership* and this *Unmistakable Imprint* we've been discussing. They go together. But this phrase is small and ordinary looking, so people often pass it right by, or else mistake it for something else.

It's this: "*and God was with him.*" There is a dimension of '*with*' that remains undiscovered by most people. But I'm about to tell you exactly how to experience this dimension, so please listen closely.

You see, though in one sense God is always *with* you because you belong to Him and His Spirit lives in you, not every believer is walking in the full measure of '*with*' that God intended. The '*with*' I am referring to only comes to those *doing what they are meant to*, David. I don't mean doing everything perfectly, but living according to the combination of one's True Identity and Special Assignment, in Partnership with God.

Too few are doing this, and it's because they missed the door. But it's not too late! Remember the story of Joseph? You know, the guy whose brothers sold him into slavery, yet he kept following God and ended up beating staggering odds, eventually becoming a powerful ruler. Joseph understood his True Identity, his Special Assignment, and how to Partner with God. As a result, God was '*with*' him in a way that left an *Unmistakable Imprint* in his life. Without rehashing the familiar story, look at this particular passage about Joseph.

> "And his master saw that the LORD was with him, and that the LORD made all that he DID to prosper in his hand." *Gen. 39:3 KJV*

Do you see the direct connection between the Lord being 'with' Joseph, him actually doing things, and successful outcomes? It was apparent, even to an ungodly master, that God was with Joseph.

How could he tell? What did he see?

It wasn't just because Joseph called himself a follower of God. The way God was 'with' him showed up in his everyday world! His boss could see it in the outcomes of Joseph's everyday life! What was entrusted to him turned out exceptionally well. The way that God was 'with' him attracted attention even from those who shunned God.

That's the Unmistakable Imprint.

We see this imprint again when Joseph had been unjustly thrown into prison. The prison keeper, another direct observer, didn't even bother to follow up on Joseph's work, because it was so exceptional.

> "The keeper of the prison paid no attention to anything that was in Joseph's charge, because the Lord was with him. And whatever he did, the Lord made it succeed." *Gen. 39:23 ESV*

There it is again. You see, David, that's what Partnership with God looks like, and that's the *'with'* that most people don't know about. If you'll Partner with God and walk through the Great Entrance to Destiny, you'll find it too.

Now listen very carefully. *The point of Partnering with God is not simply to gain wealth or success. Joseph didn't gain those until after many years in slavery and prison. The point is that there is a way to walk 'with' God where a continual flow of exceptional solutions is a hallmark in your life, an Unmistakable Imprint, no matter what you do.* David, that Way is found on the Road of your Destiny and accessed through the Great Entrance. (For the record, depending on what you are doing, exceptional solutions may lead to wealth. But God's goal for you is much bigger than that.)

Not yet fully convinced? Okay. Look at a man named Hezekiah:

> "So the Lord was with him, and Hezekiah was successful in everything he did." *2 Kings 18:7 NLT*

Now look at someone just like you:

> "David continued to succeed in everything he did, for the Lord was with him." *1 Sam. 18:14-15 NLT*

And one more…

> "…how God anointed Jesus of Nazareth with the Holy Spirit and with power. He went about doing good and healing all who were oppressed by the devil, for God was with him." *Acts 10:38 ESV*

Frankly, you won't know how vibrant your Partnership with God is until you step forward to confront a problem, a situation, or an opportunity; when you step up and lead, to DO something. But when you do, then we'll all be able to tell! We will see that God is with you in more ways than one.

I long for you to walk through the Great Entrance to Destiny and receive your own Unmistakable Imprint, David! There is just one final area we must discuss before you can fully Partner with God.

Love, the True North of Champions

> "If I had the gift of prophecy, and if I understood all of God's secret plans and possessed all knowledge, and if I had such faith that I could move mountains, but didn't love others, I would be nothing."
> *1 Cor. 13:2-3 NLT*

We'll discover more about your True Identity and Your Special Assignment as we go, but let's look at what truly guides a great champion like you. There is one last key to this Partnership that makes it all work. Without it, yours is doomed from the start.

The Key is Love.

Partnership with God is the vehicle for any and all truly meaningful achievement in life, and Love is the foundation of that Partnership: it sustains it. Without Love, nothing that we accomplish is worthwhile. Plus, you've got to be good at receiving love as well as giving it. It's the essence of your relationship with God.

And *from your relationship with God,* David, should flow a visible demonstration of what love can do. There is something amazingly intoxicating about a love story so deep that it touches lives, with or without words. (How astounding is God's love toward you and me!) So when God Himself is with you - truly with you in every way possible – this should be clearly visible even to a casual observer. Love is directly connected to the Unmistakable Imprint.

Have you ever wondered why God wants His Son married? You might think it's a funny question, but think about it. Surely He can get along without a bride? But God has decided that His Son should get married - and He's going to throw Him a party for the ages! Now marriage is a picture of love, and part of marriage is partnership. And what's incredible about this is that the Son is a perfect representation of the Father.

So Love is really the basis of your Partnership with God.

All things in this Partnership flow from love. God has rescued YOU with His love, and now you have become part of the Rescue Squad. **The reason you want to be in this Partnership is not simply to gain firepower in your efforts, but because you care about what is most important to God – people.** You care about what He cares about and you see the tremendous opportunity you have been given - to Partner with Him to touch the world while you are here!

All over the world, in every city and every country, millions upon millions of people have become separated from God and have lost hope: they are orphans, though they may not realize it. By investing your life in becoming who God has called you to be, you can dramatically impact their world. Through Partnership with Him you – yes you, David - can make a huge difference in those people's lives – right out in the everyday world.

But never forget: if you lose sight of love at any point, the impact of your Partnership will falter. So keep love in the center. Love God, and love people. That's the true north of champions.

With that, it's just about time to Partner with God. This is a very big moment. Are you ready to defeat Goliaths and accomplish great things in the everyday world?

Entering into Partnership

What are *you* going to *do with the rest of your life, David*? You can't change the past, so let's look ahead. With God as your Partner, the possibilities are amazing! In what special way will you serve the world though such a Partnership!?

Once you team up more intentionally, God won't just cheer you on. Through *you* He'll bring solutions to the world wherever you go, whatever you do! He'll answer people's questions, set them free, meet their needs, help you to serve others, and He'll be able to rule creation even more effectively. Remember, He is in charge every part of life from the Pulpit to the Marketplace, from the Family to Medicine, from Education to Government to Entertainment. But He has chosen to show His leadership in all of these areas through people willing to be His Partners.

People like you, David.

You will become a living demonstration of God's capacity in action. And others will notice. They'll see you solve difficult problems no one else can, and be amazed when answers arrive for you seemingly from nowhere. They'll see your disappointments lead to victories, your failures to success. They'll see people and projects under you managed well and turning out right. They'll be touched by your love. They'll witness improbable things. They will see opportunities appear where dead ends were predicted. They'll be surprised when you prosper without the striving, the selfish ambition, and the sorrow that so often come with "success".

> "The blessing of the LORD makes a person rich, and he adds no sorrow with it." *Prov. 10:22 NLT*

Yes, they will *see* with their own eyes a pattern of impact and outcomes that point to something beyond the regular stuff that everyone else does: they'll see an *Unmistakable Imprint*. And when they ask you what's going on, you'll know just what to say.

David, this Partnership is essential before you think about defeating Goliaths. But there are many Kingdom citizens who never get this. They live their entire lives wondering why a limitless God seems to be holding them back, when in fact He is waiting on them to enter into the Partnership He created them for.

You see, while He could do so, God tends not to steer parked cars.

I don't mean it isn't appropriate to rest and wait on the Lord for direction at times. No, my point is that some cars stay parked on the sidelines of Destiny, *or even on the road.* Some people must be hoping that the Bible means the 'Lord was with them in all they *intended* to do but never ended up doing!' Not so. Of course it's less risky to just sit on the sideline, critiquing those who are taking all the risks. But I know you don't want to waste your life doing that, David! Nor do I!

The amazing truth is this: **any ordinary Christian can do extraordinary things with God as their Partner.** So now it's your turn. God has been eagerly looking forward to this day. It's time to Partner with Him, and step out into all of life together in a new way. You will never, ever be the same, David.

Once you commit to being God's Partner in whatever you do, the possibilities in your life instantly become far greater. Until you take that step, though, you are largely working on your own in the everyday world, whether you know it or not. Of course that doesn't mean you aren't a Kingdom citizen, that He doesn't love you very much, or that you haven't been trying your best to please Him. You may have been giving it your all. It just means you have been limited to settling for far less than is possible with Him as your Partner.

Now though, you no longer have to do that. So here's the next step.

The Prayer of Partnership

Heavenly Father,

Thank you for your Grace and Wisdom.

Help me to know and live from my True Identity - the one You have given me: not a copy, an original.

Please clarify my Special Assignment from You. Give me the Courage to move toward your purpose for me. As I do so, may I learn to enjoy our relationship more than ever before. Strengthen me with Your Love, and enable me to boldly challenge the status quo when it limits what You want to do.

Help me find my Great Entrance to Destiny and walk through it.

I confess there have been times when I have gone ahead of You to do things on my own, but now I am certain that is not the way to live. Forgive me for every time I tried to do things FOR You instead of WITH You, or when I was only concerned with taking care of myself. Forgive me if I have lived like You don't care much about the everyday world. Also, please forgive me for periods when I have chased goals mostly about myself. With You, my life is so much bigger than that. Today, I ask You to expand my vision of my purpose in Your Kingdom.

I dare to consider what is possible by Partnering with You: how we can accomplish great things in life. Help me become Your Partner in a way so wonderfully effective that every day is filled with Your presence, my life is full of worthy accomplishments, others are drawn to Your greatness, and Giants are defeated - wherever we go. In our Partnership, help me pursue what is important to <u>You</u>, and to do my part according to the way You have designed and called me.

I am so grateful that You always meant for me to make a real difference in the world; that I didn't just imagine it. You put me here for a reason at this specific time, and I desire to fulfill the purpose You gave me in this generation.

Teach me to recognize the problems You want <u>me</u> to solve, the things You want <u>me</u> to do, and most importantly, the lives we can touch together. Help me lay hold of Heaven's resources to meet Earth's needs. I choose to invest my life wisely in love and partnership with You from this day forward.

From now on, we always work together.

In the mighty Name of Jesus,

Amen

Chapter 6
Key Takeaways & Giant Slayer Tips

- ❧ Rather than one-time events, your *True Identity* and *Special Assignment* are like **pathways which hold discoveries** along the way. Though you will have major moments of advance, you won't receive complete understanding in a single experience.

- ❧ There is a special place where these two paths come together. There you will find the **Great Entrance to Destiny**, a doorway to **deeper Partnership** with God.

- ❧ Others will never be influenced by God through your life the way they could be, if you are parked on the sidelines of your **Special Assignment.**

- ❧ Ideally there should be an observable, powerful connection between God's being 'with' you and what happens in your life every day. This **Unmistakable Imprint** is *the working of the Supremely Able Helper.*

- ❧ Love is the **true north of champions**, the basis of your partnership; love should always guide you, even when slaying Goliaths.

- ❧ Any ordinary Christian can **do extraordinary things with God as their Partner**. Therefore, *you* can do extraordinary things with Him as your Partner.

SECTION II
Defeating Goliaths

Armed with certain secrets, YOU WILL BE ABLE to deliver stunning impact that wins important victories and produces remarkable results.

- **Learn About Two Types of Goliaths**
- **Discover The Role Your Heart Plays In Victory**
- **Find Out Four Life-Accelerating Secrets of the Slingshot**
- **Become Skilled at Choosing Smooth Stones**
- **Meet a Remarkable, Unsung Hero**
- **Discover How to Time Your Advances Properly**
- **Learn to Win Unlikely Battles Through Inspired Decrees**

The keys are here. Take your time…

Chapter 7
Moving Into Your Promised Land

"This is my command—be strong and courageous! Do not be afraid or discouraged. For the Lord your God is with you wherever you go."
Josh. 1:9 NLT

Ever since you chose to Partner with God, great things never seemed closer. I mean it. It's as if they're right there. Your potential has always been amazing, don't get me wrong. And you've known that God had remarkable plans for you from the beginning. But now it seems like you're actually about to enter into life in a new way.

It's like you're on the threshold of greatness, David.

Did you notice a new feeling that comes over you, now and then, as your feet touch the road of Destiny - the thrilling sensation of *coming alive with the purpose of God*? It's exhilarating. If you haven't experienced it yet, as you keep walking on that path you will. So keep going; nothing replaces it.

Have you also noticed that even promises you've never let go of deep down have a tendency to rise back to the surface as you move along this way? Might as well let them bubble up.

The path seems more recognizable than it did before, too.

I guess it won't be long now before you can just stroll into your Promised Land. Let's keep going to the next lookout point and catch a view of what the land looks like from there.

Wow. That's an incredible sight. Let's pause for a minute to take it all in. It's more amazing than I imagined, yet you probably see some things that look familiar even though you haven't been this way before. Just look at all those great things right there!

Let's go!

"Wait a second... I see something. What are those?! Hey – hold up. Those look like Giants in the Land! What are they doing there? I don't get it. They don't look at all friendly, and they definitely don't look like they want us to be there. Are you sure this is the right place?"

I'm positive.

We didn't talk much about this before, David, since we weren't anywhere near here. But those things you see <u>are</u> Giants on the Road of your Destiny, blocking the way to the great things God has promised. They are standing in other people's way too, not just yours.

So who's going to step up and take them on?

"Great... Just what I needed. More resistance. I thought you told me I was just about to enter a whole new level of achievement that I've been dreaming about for a long time. But this is just more of the same old life, filled with challenges and obstacles. And anyway, I'm sick and tired of metaphorical stuff. Life has enough real problems."

I understand your frustration, David, but the big difference here is that you're about to bust a Giant in the chops. You weren't before. So the results will be quite different.

"Really? Tell me more..."

The fact is, if someone doesn't step up to them at the right time and in the correct manner, the Giants won't budge. So who's going to, and how should they do it?

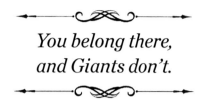

You belong there, and Giants don't.

Remember when I told you that most people's Special Assignment does <u>not</u> revolve around living at Base Camp? That we all have a role there, but only a select few are full-time, or should even want to be? For most of us, our Special Assignment is to venture into another part of the everyday world on a crucial mission – a mission we are well-equipped for.

And yes, it looks like the Road of *your* Destiny, David, is leading you smack dab *into* the everyday world, not away from it; and into a section filled with Giants!

To have any hope of defeating them, *you first need to realize that you truly belong there - and they don't!* That's the first step. I know it sounds simplistic, but it's vital. Unfortunately, most among us don't even grasp this first step to slaying Giants. You must keep it in mind, though: **You belong there - and the Giants DON'T.**

Let's keep going, and your mission will become clearer.

So you're on this road of your Destiny, starting to move well, and it carries you into Business, or Government, or Media, or Education, or Medicine, or Social Justice, or the Arts, or some other area. Instead of trying to take a different route, you recognize that God wants you there because He has plans for each area, and you carry a part of His plan. There are people He wants you to help there, and specific things He wants you to accomplish.

I understand, everyone functions in the everyday world: it's a basic part of life. My point is that *few Kingdom citizens understand the full scope of the mission they are on WHILE THERE.* They get part of it, but not enough. They don't realize that they have been sent there on Special Assignment, and that they carry a mandate from Heaven to help make things right in that certain part of our everyday world.

So when they look around and see big problems, how messed up things are, and the big bad guys who are in control - instead of realizing the true difference they can make in the marketplace as Giant Slayers – sadly, they decide instead to just live normal, ordinary lives.

Your New Look

So let me get this straight. You're finally going to head directly *into* the everyday world *to fulfill your Destiny* - not just to pass the time while you wait for something more 'spiritual' to come along?

This is great news! I don't know what to say… Wow!

There's something else, David. While I watched you take these last few steps, I noticed a different look in your eye. I saw you starting to carry yourself like an actual Giant Slayer, ready to step up to big challenges wherever they appear. You didn't look like you were going to back down at all. You followed the road of Destiny here, and God Himself gave you your Special Assignment: it seems to be coming together!

"But what about the Giants?"

Yeah, those pesky Giants.

Two Kinds of Goliaths

OK, you're ready to forge ahead, but there appear to be obstacles in the way. Fine.

What do they look like?

Why are they there?

What, if anything, should <u>you</u> do about them?

There are certainly some big problems in this world. Really big problems. Everyone knows it, but most people don't want to look too closely. Strangely, a lot of these people are Kingdom citizens. I mean we *talk* about the problems sometimes, but most often it's only so we can steer clear of them. Some of us want to address them, but usually our efforts fall short. We can't quite seem to create the change that we believe in our hearts is possible.

So let's examine these problems for a minute. I mean *really* look around at what's happening in the everyday world. What catches your eye? Major Giants, the ones we call Goliaths, are mostly at work in areas that influence many people, places like the Arts, Media & Entertainment, Science & Medicine, Business & Technology, Government, Education, Family, and Spirituality & Religion.

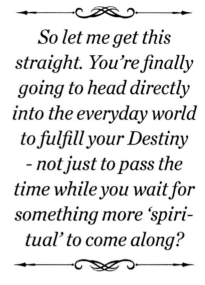

So let me get this straight. You're finally going to head directly into the everyday world to fulfill your Destiny - not just to pass the time while you wait for something more 'spiritual' to come along?

David, now that you know <u>you are supposed to be where you are and Giants are not</u>, there is no reason to ignore them. Quite the opposite, in fact. God's ways are supreme in all of those areas, even when His people working there don't know how to tap into His wisdom for winning great victories.

The First Type of Goliaths

Maybe you see Hunger or Corruption or a malicious illness causing great suffering. Perhaps what stands out to you are the huge amounts of money moving toward people who lavish it on themselves and support ungodly causes. Maybe it's people mistreating other people, families in distress, or marriages on the rocks. Or possibly you notice an entire group of people who believe some major untruth that is tearing them apart. Maybe there is a particular section of town or your region that never seems to get ahead economically. Maybe you watch beautiful, valuable things that God has created being misused, or a cycle of unrealized potential due to poor Education. Perhaps you observe people creating beautiful things or doing great feats, but taking full personal credit without giving God any. Maybe you see terrorists threatening innocent lives.

Maybe you see drugs capturing young people, small businesses failing unnecessarily, or television programs that lure people away from healthy relationships. Maybe you see leaders making decisions and setting policies which create unjust or counterproductive solutions. Or maybe you see a powerful method for influencing people being used to destroy them instead of to empower them. Maybe you see Poverty or Racism or Sexism or Atheism. Perhaps you see a technological problem that can be solved with a new approach. Maybe you see poor leadership, great hardship, or clear injustice.

I'm not certain what you see from where you stand. But there definitely are some Giants in the Land: *Giant Problems*. That's the most important kind of Goliath. They are so big, who would really dare to challenge them? I know people sometimes try, but usually it doesn't work. After all, *daring* is one thing, *delivering* is another.

But no matter what, remember what I told you: *It's us who belong there, and the Giant Problems that don't.* Make sure that sinks in, because if you ever forget it, you will never defeat a Goliath.

Now try looking near the path of *your* Special Assignment. Can you see any Giant Problems from there? I wonder.

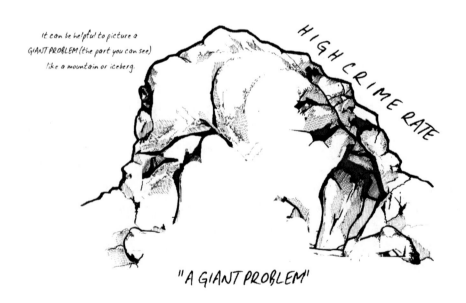

It can be helpful to picture a
GIANT PROBLEM (the part you can see)
like a mountain or iceberg.

HIGH CRIME RATE

"A GIANT PROBLEM"

"Wait, I have a question. If God is really in charge of everything, why are so many of the Giant Problems so big and seemingly unmovable, no matter what anyone does? They just tower over everybody as if there's no way to stop them."

Ah, that's a very good question, David.

The Second Type of Goliaths

That leads us to the second type of Goliaths: spiritual Goliaths. *Spiritual Giants.* These are the kind that few people understand, and most don't even want to discuss. So we will, because understanding this second type is often a key to solving a Giant Problem; you'll soon see why.

> "Our fight is not against people on the earth, but against the rulers and authorities and the powers of this world's darkness, against the spiritual powers of evil in the heavenly world." *Eph. 6:12 NCV*

Spiritual Giants are unseen spiritual forces bent on opposing God, and destroying and robbing people. Their abilities are indeed formidable, yet also limited. They try to deceive people and influence them to do the Giants' will. They try to make evil look good, and they lie about God. They use their power to steal, kill, and destroy. They have actually been defeated already, but just not completely evicted yet.

"Why not?"

Good question...

The fate of Spiritual Giants is much more certain and more immediate than we realize. But since our short lifetimes are one of the main measures of time we can relate to, when things don't change immediately or within just a few years, we often wonder what is taking so long, or if anything is actually changing. God, however, lives outside our concept of time.

In the meantime, this type of Goliath hangs around causing major problems all over the earth. *They especially don't like the way that God wants to clean house, and they certainly don't want you to help Him.* They'd also prefer that you don't bother to learn any more about them.

"Uh, you know what? I just realized that I have something very

important I need to do right now. We can discuss this part later."

You have something better to do?? You mean you just want to skip this part because you're not even sure whether you believe in Spiritual Giants. Nonsense, David; you need to pay close attention to this. Hidden here are some vital keys to fulfilling your Destiny.

Whether you believe in them or not, the Inspired Guidebook makes it very clear that Spiritual Giants are real, and they affect both you and everyone else in the everyday world. *Though there are various types, we will focus on the larger spiritual Giants which affect many people at once: the Goliaths.* These are the ones that must fall.

Why Spiritual Giants are in the Everyday World

"What are Spiritual Giants doing in the everyday world? If they are spiritual beings mad at God or something, wouldn't they be mostly focused on attacking our Base Camps and just messing up Kingdom citizens? I mean, that seems to me like what they would do. But I'm still not sure I understand this why-they-are-in-the-everyday-world-thing."

I'll tell you a secret. *Spiritual Giants are already certain they have no hope of winning at Base Camp.*

This doesn't mean they don't try to mess things up there sometimes, but it's far less of a focus than most people think. However, Giants do try to keep our thinking small enough so we won't confront them out in the everyday world, that's for sure. Because without much strategic interference from Kingdom citizens, Giants can more comfortably pursue their goals, running around largely unchecked. So they do, wreaking havoc. That's one reason why things are so messed up in places. Soon we'll get to *how* they wreak their havoc. But since they basically work to destroy *all* people - not just professing Christians - Spiritual Giants prefer direct access to greater masses; that's why they focus their efforts heavily in the everyday world.

As well, many of the best natural means to influence people and capture their loyalties are created and controlled in the everyday world. So to Giants, working in the everyday world more than at Base

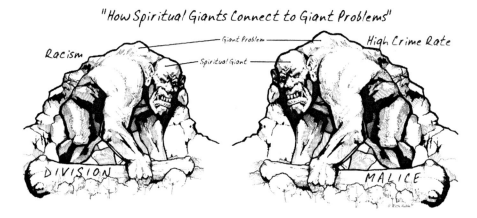

"How Spiritual Giants Connect to Giant Problems"

Racism — Giant Problem — High Crime Rate — Spiritual Giant —

DIVISION

MALICE

Camp is simply 'fishing where the fish are'.

Unfortunately, in vital areas where Spiritual Giants have chosen to dig in, most of God's people on the other hand have been taught that the everyday world doesn't even matter. So we've totally missed what these Spiritual Giants are up to. Or if we know, we're not sure how to deal with them. *So even though cooperating with each other and with the aid of the Supremely Able Helper is one of the best ways to disrupt the activities of Spiritual Giants*, we fail to use these means where Giants are most active. That's a major reason why their current hold on many areas of society is so commanding. Fortunately, it's also temporary.

How Spiritual Giants Work

Spiritual Giants love to mislead people and spread ideas about God that are untrue. Once a person believes their lies, that person is not only affected personally, but then can also be used spread the lies to others - often without even knowing it. Spiritual Giants like to bind people to things which at first appear desirable, using forces such as Greed, Fear, Lust, Pride, and Selfish Ambition. But in the end, that bond to what seemed harmless proves destructive.

Spiritual Giants even work to control specific regions and organizations, and they can support the advance of evil with spiritual powers we don't fully understand. But we don't have to.

What really matters is not complicated teaching exposing all they do, but simply understanding that they exist, and being aware that in many cases a Giant Problem can be connected to a Spiritual Giant. That connection does make the Giant Problem more difficult to defeat, so it's important to know. It's even more important to know that God's power - which is with <u>you</u>, David! - is far greater than the power of all Spiritual Giants combined.

So don't fret.

You Can Run but You Can't Hide

Now of course we humans are plenty capable of causing major problems just by ourselves, but many *major* issues in the everyday world can be traced to the work of Spiritual Giants. Let me show you a few examples of what these connections can look like.

Do you see that large group of artists who create magnificent works - the best of their kind - and yet openly speak out against God, deny that their talents are gifts from Him, and instead give credit to other powers? Why are so many in that group affected like that? And how are they able to have such a major impact on society? Looks like there might be more to it.

Do you see that popular local official who convinces the people in your area that taking the lives of unborn children does not dishonor God? It's remarkable how much more effective she is at advancing her message than God's family is at saving lives. It seems like things just seem to go her way, and she persuades lots of people to believe like she does. Why does it seem like that will never change? Maybe there is more to it.

Until a Giant Slayer shows up, that Giant Problem will continue. Where are you, David?

Do you see the moral devastation created by that Media Company that is influencing the minds of millions through their well produced, hugely successful films - films that dishonor God? Then they use the profits to promote even more ideas and groups that deny Him, thus expanding their influence.

We Kingdom citizens often talk from a distance about what that company is doing wrong, but we can't make much headway against the actual problem. Perhaps there's a Spiritual Giant at work behind the scenes. And instead of finding a way to attain leadership positions in the industry, thus being able to make films that creatively communicate better storylines - combining our beliefs with our actions - we make excuses about how filmmaking is unspiritual. Are there any Giant Slayers out there?

How about the spreading disease that affects millions, seeming to deny that even God can stop it? Is that just someone else's problem? It will continue to steal precious lives in its path until the right David comes along.

Do you see that large and growing business that uses its influence to advance ideas that discredit God, yet it is operated more effectively than many companies run by Kingdom citizens? Many unbelievers are using their God-given skills more diligently and creatively than we are. Where are the even more successful companies led by people like you, David? Those Kingdom citizens who follow God without compromise, partner with Him to do great things, steward wealth to creatively advance His Kingdom, and add great value to the world?

Do you see the hardships facing that country with the corrupt government? Its leaders are liars who oppress and steal from their own people, acting as if nothing can stop them. Do you see the pride that lures children in, as athletes of winning teams parade around the field as if their ability came from themselves alone, refusing to give honor to the One who created them with such talent?

If you look around a little, you'll start to recognize combinations of Giant Problems and Spiritual Giants. They are right around the corner in your community, affecting schools, businesses, key leaders, and neighborhoods. Some have larger effects than that. Without realizing it, you may even be facing Giants in something you are trying to do.

Think of the Giant Problem as the part you can see with your eyes, David, like the tip of an iceberg, and the Spiritual Giant as the part of the iceberg below the water.

Why Mess With Spiritual Giants?

"Now just a minute. I thought this kind of stuff was completely God's work. Besides, His Son has already defeated the power of evil. I'm not messing with Spiritual Giants. Are you crazy?"

No, David. But here's the part you're missing. It's hidden in that special message you read before about Spiritual Giants. Reread the first two words.

> "Our fight is not against people on the earth, but against the rulers and authorities and the powers of this world's darkness, against the spiritual powers of evil in the heavenly world." *Eph. 6:12 NCV*

Whose fight?

"Our fight".

Yes... *our* fight.

Though the overall battle is the Lord's, we are also in the war against Spiritual Giants. *You must know this: you are in this fight and affected by it - whether you want to be or not.* So when a Giant Problem is blocking the path to your Special Assignment, David, you need to be aware that a Spiritual Giant could be the real cause of the problem, the real 'power' behind it.

Dealing with Spiritual Giants

But don't worry. You have been given divine potential to disrupt the activities of Spiritual Giants. That is, when you work with the Supremely Able Helper and in Partnership with God. Also, it's very helpful to work together with like-minded people to secure total victory. There is strength in numbers and agreement. We'll talk more about this when you train to use your Slingshot.

As you start to recognize these signs I've told you about, instead of marveling at how many things in this world are so messed up, you can be prepared for action. While others avoid getting involved solving the Giant Problems of our day – as if they have more important things to do - you won't stand for it.

Mere spiritual Giants cannot intimidate you unless you allow them to, David, no matter how imposing they may seem. So don't allow them to. When they gaze in your direction and realize that you know your True Identity and are teamed up with God, they'll think twice before messing with you. When God arises, His enemies scatter!

But beware. *Stick to the path of your Special Assignment, the Road of Destiny. Go after Giant Problems you encounter there, but don't randomly pick fights with every Giant you see.* That's unwise.

Defeating Smaller Giants

One last thing before we move on. So far we have focused on defeating Goliaths, and for good reason. By conquering *them*, you change the world, which is part of *your* Special Assignment. That, after all, is a major focus of our time together. Yet on the Road of Destiny there are also many smaller, more personal battles. Some are merely practical problems, while others have spiritual roots.

But they are real too, and not handled properly they can still stop you. *If you're not careful, something that is really not a Goliath can become like one.* You can't allow that to happen. Otherwise, next thing you know you'll look down and the Road of Destiny will no longer be under your feet. Instead, to keep moving forward, use smaller Giants for practice; view those personal battles as preparation for greater ones. A Giant Slayer deals with smaller sized Giants *on the way* to defeating true Goliaths and helping others. The secrets in this book will also help you deal with those Goons.

When we start to view life the way we should, and realize that even the everyday world belongs to God - and that we can Partner with Him to accomplish great things in it – look out! Though Giant Problems can loom large, and Spiritual Giants work to keep your thinking narrow and block your way, you, David, are a true Giant Slayer!

So next, we'll prepare a part of you that's crucial for victory – your heart.

Chapter 7

Key Takeaways & Giant Slayer Tips

- One of the first keys of a Giant Slayer is understanding that **you are supposed to be here**; Giants are not.

- You have been sent into the everyday world on Special Assignment, and **you carry a mandate from Heaven** to help make things right in your arena.

- There are two types of Goliaths: **Giant Problems & Spiritual Giants**. Giant Problems are significant issues which affect large numbers of people in the everyday world. Spiritual Giants are unseen spiritual forces bent on destroying people, robbing them, and opposing God.

- Most of the best methods to capture people's attention and influence them are operating **in the everyday world**.

- A **Giant Problem can be connected to a Spiritual Giant**. That connection makes the Giant Problem much more difficult to solve.

- The **fight against spiritual Giants** is not just God's, it is also ours.

Chapter 8
Heart of a Giant Slayer

"O my son, give me your heart. May your eyes take delight in following my ways." Prov. 23:26 NLT

Does it take heart to slay Giants? Interesting question.

If so, what kind of heart? Isn't it just a cold-blooded act, a one-time thing? There you are one day, charging toward a massive beast, and then it's all over in an instant. You live off that one victory for the rest of your life, thanking God for at least one moment in the sun.

No David, it's definitely not like that; there's much more to it.

A Giant Slayer is a person you must develop into. As you grow into those shoes, when the time is right you'll be ready defeat Goliaths and then go on to accomplish even greater things. However, to be prepared to conquer these Giants as they appear, you need to submit to training in different areas of your life. Your Heavenly Father knows the road ahead, and He is preparing you to walk victoriously along yours.

But one of the greatest challenges you'll face on that route is not outside you, it's within your heart. What goes on in the invisible realm of your heart can make all the difference in the world. What's more, how your heart is changing is often imperceptible to others. You can go weeks, months, and even years when - on the surface - it seems like nothing is changing, but deep down major changes are happening. It can be tempting, therefore, to shortcut the process, and also easy to make wrong judgments about other people based on how they appear.

So let's look deeper for a minute, into the heart of a Giant Slayer.

You already know that love is the true north of champions, so love's got to be in the heart. Of course. But what else should be in your heart? Are there any other things you'll need to slay Giants? Yes.

"*What, exactly?*"

Devotion, Honor, and Valor, for starters. And that's not all. Humility, Generosity, and Kindness are also important. Service too.

"*But what does any of that have to do with slaying Giants?*"

Here's what.

A Giant Slayer's heart is a Kingdom Heart. A Kingdom Heart honors the King, honors the Kingdom, the ways of its King, and others in the Kingdom. As a Giant Slayer, you're devoted to your King, which means not only loving Him and His allies - but *opposing the King's enemies*. It comes with the territory, like it or not. For many people, misunderstanding what this means is a major reason they are not among the King's Mighty Warriors – yet.

To become a Giant Slayer you must be willing to fight the battles the King sends you into. It's not something to take lightly or pass over, David. In fact, you can master everything in this book, yet if you miss this truth you will never slay one Goliath. Sadly, there are scores of Kingdom citizens marching to the beat of their own individual drums, with no regard for the King's strategic commands.

Can you imagine *any* Kingdom where none of its citizens are willing to stand up for the Kingdom, none who care about the King's concerns or follow His commands? That's no Kingdom. It's chaos. It won't last.

Your King has some enemies, and He's calling you to act boldly as a Kingdom citizen. Remember that these enemies are primarily Giants in the Land, not people. So simply doing natural things like grabbing a sword, trying to prosper, or building your influence won't get the job done. You must combine spiritual and natural things to slay Giants. (For some reason, it's common to excel in one or the other, but rare to do both effectively.)

Real Giant Slayers don't appear on the scene simply to become wealthy or well-known, but for a higher purpose. They rise to face a specific challenge...

Sadly, far too many Kingdom citizens prefer to let someone else defend the King's honor. Even with Him right at their side filling their hearts with Courage, they retreat. They can't identify with His Honor - or maybe they are preoccupied with their own.

But for Giant Slayers, the King's battle is not optional, even when others opt out. In fact, a Giant Slayer rises up when others back down. This heart of Valor to displace the King's enemies is vital, yet rare. But you, David, I think you have one!

"Do you really believe I'll be able to defeat Goliaths?"

Yes, of course you will, David.

Now you also need to consider this: Real Giant Slayers don't appear on the scene simply to become wealthy or well known, but for a higher purpose. They rise to face a specific challenge; they step forward because they see injustice and can't ignore it; they spot opportunity and are willing to risk failure; they hear the cry of the lacking and work to supply them; they see the lost and bring Hope; they recognize Giants in the Land and won't allow them to roam free, harming people without consequences. That is the heart of a Giant Slayer.

So be very careful that you aren't deceived by mere outward appearances. Because Giant Slayers ultimately do noticeable things, they are sometimes confused with people who have <u>only</u> outward accomplishments but no Kingdom heart.

The Story of Great Friend

I once had a Great Friend. Great Friend was cool, business savvy, and involved at our Local Base Camp; he sometimes donated his financial and other leadership skills to serve there. He had a beautiful wife and children, a lovely home, and a strong extended family; I admired and respected Great Friend.

Some of it was simply the way Great Friend carried himself: he was so confident in his business dealings, and he had built an impressive business enterprise. He had the kind of authority everyone wishes they had. He was generous too, and a welcoming host. When you went to his house you never needed to bring anything, and the spread was fantastic. He always figured out in advance a couple of things you liked and he made sure they were there.

With Great Friend around, I felt energized.

When his company began experiencing some turmoil, he calmly weathered the storm, and I admired his determination in the face of such difficulty. As weeks of turmoil dragged into months, it was a humbling experience for him, but Great Friend refused to give up.

Things just kept falling apart, though, and patching them became his full-time job. The pressure built to a point that it began affecting his daily life. Great Friend became obsessed with saving his company to such a degree that he began taking cell phone calls in the middle of meals - not just once or twice, but all the time. Family outings and friendly get-togethers became a series of apologies about his having to take care of other, more important matters.

Then I got a call from another Great Friend, the Faithful Leader of my Local Base Camp.

"Rick, I have a very important question to ask you," said Faithful Leader. "It's confidential, so please keep it that way."

"Okay," I replied, hearing an unusually urgent tone in his voice.

"Did you know that Great Friend spent the last few days on that 'business trip' actually with some woman he used to know - but not his wife?"

The words were English but didn't make sense to me.

"What?!? Say that again, I don't think I'm following you." He repeated his statement. As he did, that sick feeling you get, like when news of a dramatic bad turn of events finally registers in your brain, stormed into the room uninvited. My face flushed.

"You mean MY Great Friend? There is no way!" I shot back, half-disbelieving. "Are you certain?"

"His wife just called me, and she seems absolutely certain," said Faithful Leader.

"Here's what I want to ask you," he continued. "Did you see ANY signs of this at all? I mean, you guys used to spend a lot of time together. I'm just scratching my head because I didn't see this coming and I thought maybe, at least between the two of us, maybe you sensed something was wrong. I just have no idea how I could have missed something like this."

"Faithful Leader, I'm at a loss on this one. I like to think that I recognize telltale signs before it's too late, especially with people close to me, but this makes me wonder. I did ask him about the trip, but his reply made it sound like just a few days of ordinary business with a boat trip thrown in, and we left it at that."

"If it's true", Faithful Leader went on, "this whole thing is deeply disturbing on two levels. First, what this does to his wife and kids, even himself, and also, that you and I could be so close to someone *and not have any earthly idea what is really going on in their heart*. It's just awful and alarming at the same time."

"You've got that right," I said.

"Well, I have a meeting with him soon and I'll ask him point blank. I hope it's not true, but his wife sounded convinced. And she said she has proof," Faithful Leader said finally.

At their meeting, Great Friend assured Faithful Leader that the accusation was off base.

"Phew; maybe it wasn't true after all!" I thought.

A few days later though, in a surprising confession after repeated denials directly to Faithful Leader and others, Great Friend finally admitted the affair.

"Well, delayed honesty is better than continued lies," I thought. "This is terrible, but they have a strong marriage; they can work this out. We'll stand with them."

But Great Friend didn't want to work it out. So instead of working to find the humility and repentance to move past such a huge mistake, he instead continued in the way his heart had already chosen. I couldn't believe my ears as now he supposedly didn't love his wife and hadn't for a while, and he was ready to simply walk out and leave his wife, daughter, and newborn baby.

"This is blatant deception," I thought. "He can come to his senses if it hasn't completely taken over his heart. Let's pray! I know Great Friend, and he's not one to give up easily; maybe there is still hope!"

Friends and family prayed and believed, but after a brief time, the once remarkable couple split up. Great Friend didn't want to talk to me and I didn't reach out much to him; all our plans to do things together evaporated. Soon remarried, Once-Great-Friend has continued to pursue his number one priority: business success. Within just a few years, Once-Great-Friend became one of the richer people I have ever personally known, and at last report, his annual salary exceeds what most people make in their entire lifetime (or even two).

Has Once-Great-Friend ever slain a Goliath? I can't say for sure, but I doubt it. Unless his heart has changed - which is possible, and I pray it has - all the wealth and influence in the world can't help slay even one real Goliath.

Remember: **The heart of a Giant Slayer is a Kingdom heart; don't be fooled by outward appearances.** David, I have to ask you, *why are you really doing what you're doing right now, anyway*? What's motivating you? Is deep love for your King filling you with desire to carry out His Special Assignment for you with Honor, or is something else magnetizing you?

To slay Giants, David, you must honor God in your heart. Of course our hearts are vast territories, and it's not easy to submit completely to

Him. You have to work at it, daily; we all do. And since so much of the process happens just between you and God, when no one else is keeping track, it can be tempting to take shortcuts.

Resist the urge! Sometimes it's not easy, I know.

But when your heart becomes set on things it shouldn't, this acts like a slow poison, turning you away from your destiny as a true Giant Slayer. You'll become much weaker than it may appear on the outside. You can always get back on track, of course, but don't wait. If something's not right, I'd talk it over with the King right now if I were you. In matters of the heart, you can fool others for a time, but eventually what's inside comes to the surface.

Also know this: if you have been making right choices, David, doing what's right when no one is looking – making the tough calls - this has been strengthening you to accomplish great things in the days ahead. Sometimes you've just got to tend sheep and practice your harp faithfully for as long as it takes for God to train you and prepare your heart.

Allow your heart to be conquered first by God, and ultimately you too will become a conqueror.

Chapter 8

Key Takeaways & Giant Slayer Tips

☑ What goes on in the **invisible realm of your heart** can make all the difference in the world. For one thing, your motives, which are of great interest to God, live there.

☑ A Giant Slayer is a person **you must develop into**. It won't happen overnight.

☑ For a Giant Slayer, the King's battle is not optional, even when others opt out. Continual willingness to **engage in the fight**, to displace the King's enemies and advance the King's interests, is *absolutely required*. Inability or unwillingness to grasp this disqualifies many.

☑ A Giant Slayer does not appear on the scene to become wealthy or well known, but **for a higher purpose**.

☑ A Giant Slayer **honors** the King, those He has placed in authority, and other people.

☑ A Giant Slayer **resists the urge** to take shortcuts when no one else is looking.

Chapter 9
The Secrets of the Slingshot

"…with the right strategy you can wage war…" *Prov. 24:6 GOD'S WORD*

Mustering the courage to stand up to a fearsome Giant is, by itself, a remarkable feat; few people ever go that far. Yet *marching bravely into* such a battle, David, and *emerging victorious* – those are two completely different matters! Life is full of too many near misses and valiant, but failed, efforts; don't you think? How would you like to see more improbable upsets, where 'unlikely' heroes (who are really the good guys) actually <u>win</u>? Better yet, how would *you* like to become one of those champions?

Fantastic! Of course you would!

However, since boldness alone won't carry the day, it raises questions such as: what else exactly does it require to defeat a Goliath? Can you *really* take him on and win? And - is it even appropriate for an ordinary Kingdom citizen to dream of slaying Giants!?

David, may the following words land deep in your heart, and remain there forever as a challenge and an encouragement to you: EVERY Kingdom citizen has the potential to slay Giants!! Even in your toughest times, never forget that this is your Destiny! You were created with the capacity to accomplish truly remarkable things with God, even when all the odds seem stacked against you.

All the same, defeating a Giant does require special knowledge and craft: *secrets,* if you will, for Giant Slayers. In this chapter, some of those secrets are precisely what we will discuss. Yet here's a strange thing. Since these secrets are only meant for those warriors truly willing to step into the ring with Giants and thus change the world, *other readers will struggle to grasp the full significance of what's here* (even though it's all written in plain English). For those readers, these secrets will appear too obvious, too general, not spiritual enough - or even too spiritual. For whatever reason, without even realizing the huge mistake they are making, those readers will discard the very same set of principles that others will use to win amazing victories. For them, sadly, no help is here.

But for you, David, it's an entirely different story. Though God cannot be reduced to principles, *He does have secrets which lead to remarkable advance, for those who will listen.* So I submit these to you to consider and explore.

Get ready to accelerate in ways only possible with Him!

The Four Main Keys

Near the beginning of this book I mentioned that I once stumbled upon a Slingshot. I also said that it looked quite ordinary, but it turned out to be more valuable than I ever imagined. Now it's time to explore what's so unusual about a plain-looking Slingshot, and how such a weapon can help *you* slay Giants.

There are four main keys involved; each key is powerful all by itself - but using them *together* results in far, far greater effect. I'll refer to these keys collectively as the *Slingshot Principles.* And these principles will not only help you defeat Goliaths, David, they will help you greatly advance many things you attempt in life.

With that, let's take a look at the four main Slingshot Principles:

1. **The Key of Prayer**

2. **The Key of Courage**

3. **The Key of Skill**

4. **The Key of Unconventional Tactics**

"What's so special about <u>this</u> list?"

I understand, David: this list probably looks quite like others you've seen, and its contents seem familiar enough. Even so, I advise you to hold on to it for safe-keeping.

<u>Because these keys are not nearly as ordinary as they might first appear.</u>

For now, let me simply suggest that they are divinely inspired, that they have remained largely untapped until this time, and that *they release special properties when combined in certain ways.* In other words, there is far more here than meets the eye! (You'll learn more about each of these mysterious attributes later in this chapter.) Let me further advise you that one of their most interesting properties is this - *these keys only produce maximum effect when wielded by Kingdom citizens.*

You might already be wondering how each key applies to your pursuits and Destiny, or mulling over which keys seem more or less important to you. Maybe you feel as though you already know how to use each one, or perhaps you have tried a couple and thought they were nothing special. Again, I understand your feelings. But David, I pray that, whatever your previous experience has been with these keys, you will allow yourself the freedom to explore them anew – and that you will be open to learning their hidden secrets.

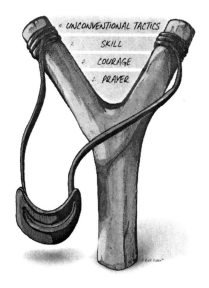

One thing is for sure: Giants would much rather you forget all about this chapter and go on to something else! You might have been hearing their comments already without realizing it, in thoughts like: "Maybe I should just skim through this part? After all, I know a good bit about all of these keys already. I'll just skip ahead to some more important section, and read this one later."

Proceed with care, David - and just maybe, you'll be extremely surprised at what you discover.

#1: The Key of PRAYER

"...The earnest prayer of a righteous person has great power and produces wonderful results." *Jam. 5:16 NLT*

PRAYER CONNECTS YOU WITH GOD IN MULTIPLE, STRATEGIC WAYS; IT ATTRACTS HIS STRENGTH.

Prayer is necessary to defeat a real Giant. But too often this key isn't used to its full effect – especially where most Giants roam free: in the Marketplace.

"What kind of Prayer? How much? When? Besides, every believer knows about Prayer and prays regularly and effectively, don't they?"

No, David, too often they don't. But more importantly, let's make sure *you* know how to use this key to the full extent.

Through Prayer you connect with God in ways that influence the outcomes of what you attempt in life, and you learn His desires and strategy. *Prayer is an incredible opportunity to access Heaven's resources to meet Earth's needs - and to usher in God's plans!* Yes, it's also a sacred time of communing, deep relationship, and much more. But remember, here we are talking specifically about Prayer's role in Giant Slaying and exceptional achievement.

Those Kingdom citizens who don't learn to pray effectively are spiritually weakened, and are likely to be beaten by almost any Giant. When you step up to face a real Goliath, you don't want to be limited to human ability alone: that would be very foolish. Why would you ever choose to face a Giant all by yourself? But people do it all the time in the everyday world.

Fervent Prayer, on the other hand, connects you with God and attracts His strength. Prayer invites God into your circumstances to do what only He can! Also, as you talk things over with Him, He often will show you more effective ways of doing things. But you have to ask, and then really listen for His response. You need to communicate with Him. Talk to Him. Make specific requests about the outcome of things you are doing. Ask Him regularly what He wants you to do and how you should do it.

Don't Get Robbed; Broaden Your Scope of Prayer

We're not talking only about praying for the lost in that far country, or missionaries you know, or a very sick person, or a troubled family member, or when you meet in small groups, or about things you do at Base Camp, or before meals or at bedtime. Of course those Prayers are important, but *Prayer is not simply for Base Camp activities and a few emergency situations; it's for everything.*

You already know Prayer works, David. And yet perhaps, like many of us, you still haven't found how to use this Key in the everyday world to its greatest potential. For example, do you remember Daniel and his friends, how they excelled?

"And in every matter of wisdom and understanding, concerning which the king inquired of them, he found them ten times better than all the magicians and enchanters that were in all his realm." *Dan. 1:20 ASV*

And do you also remember that the Inspired Guidebook plainly reveals that God is no respecter of persons? (Meaning He doesn't play favorites.) So if God was willing to cause Daniel and his friends to be <u>10 times more qualified in matters of wisdom & understanding in the everyday world</u>, would He do the same for you? Of course He would! What an incredible realization!! Yet without Prayer, such a blessing will likely remain unclaimed. So access this amazing provision by asking God to release such favor in *your* life, and expecting Him to do so - as you are willing to position yourself to make use of it for Kingdom purposes.

Without proper Prayer you are far less effective, less informed, less confident, and more vulnerable - whether you are in the boardroom, the washroom, the White House – or even behind the pulpit. Your Partner knows exactly which tactics expose a Giant's weakness and which will ensure victory on multiple fronts. But if you don't take time to ask Him, especially at key points along the way, you invite defeat.

Here is what many un-successful Giant Slayers miss: they do not pray with significant enough determination or consistency about things they are trying to do in the everyday world, because they don't see those things as spiritual enough.

Here is what many unsuccessful Giant Slayers miss: they don't pray with significant enough determination or consistency about things they are trying to do in the everyday world, because they don't see those things as 'spiritual' enough. That belief robs them of one of the great difference-makers available to every Kingdom Citizen, in any arena.

But the Inspired Guidebook is clear on this matter:

"Work willingly at whatever you do, as though you were working for the Lord rather than for people." *Col. 3:23 NLT*

And your work falls under the

category of something you do: therefore your work is spiritual. End of story. **Lack of effective communication with God in the everyday world contributes heavily to Kingdom citizens experiencing far less than what is possible in life.**

What does it look like when you settle for less? It means that a promotion you could have had or an election you should have won, the relationship you hoped for, the proposal you should have landed, the message you should have passed along to that person, the problem you could have solved, the breakthrough you expected, the miracle you should have delivered, the impact you could have made, the dream that should have materialized and the victory won – these all remain out of reach. And Giants you could have slain still stand in your way. Life stays frustratingly below what you dream is possible and what you believe could be.

But effective Prayer can change all that.

Just because you are God's child doesn't mean there won't be difficult times in your life. But when troubles arrive, a Giant Slayer presses through. When it comes to worthwhile projects, difficult problems, new ideas, and big dreams that involve your time and attention in the everyday world - *if it's worth doing, it's worth praying about.*

Your life in the marketplace is important, David. It's where most of us are called to be. God never intended your activities there, specifically work, to be a waste of time. I hope you know that. You are not treading water, hoping for something more 'spiritual' to come along. *You don't have to go anywhere else to walk closely with God and see His incredible power work through your life.* Start where you are. You are already in the middle of God's Battle for the hearts and minds of people - RIGHT WHERE YOU ARE - facing Giants. God wants to be involved with you every step of the way on a glorious shared journey as your Father, Helper, and Partner. The only time it gets really scary is when you try to rush ahead on your own. So don't.

So Many Rich Benefits!

As you spend time with God in Prayer, your heart becomes more able to hear His voice more frequently, and your relationship grows. Rather than merely an activity, Prayer becomes more like a communication channel which once only worked occasionally, but now is open much more often. Your awareness of God's presence increases. You even find yourself *not always asking for things* when you are together, but simply enjoying His company - and knowing that He enjoys yours. You begin receiving direction more clearly, even while 'doing other things'. As you read the Inspired Guidebook, it comes alive more than before and transforms you more deeply. The desire to pray bubbles up from inside you, rather than simply as a result of reminding yourself what's on the 'Good Kingdom Citizen' checklist.

But here is one of the greatest benefits to praying more. As you begin to invest more time into communicating with God, *you begin caring more about the things He cares about.* As a result, more of the stuff you dream of begins to take its cue from His heart. And that, David, changes everything! Deep down, your reasons for doing things become different. What you want to accomplish now becomes infused with the Mission of Heaven. Not because you are trying with all your effort to make it so, but because He's working in you. God rubs off on you when you spend time with Him.

> "...for it is God who works in you both to will and to do for His good pleasure." *Phil. 2:13 NKJV*

When your heart becomes more like His, David, the possibilities skyrocket. Then you can really think big! You can dream WITH God according to your True Identity and Special Assignment. Giants that others fear become fair game for you.

Valuing the Prayers of Others

But as important as it is for YOU to pray, the Key of Prayer is not simply about what you can do alone, or even with God's help. It's not simply the prayers *you* pray that turn this Key, or scheduling a prayer time, or meeting with a prayer group. To use it fully you are going to have to raise the overall value you place on Prayer, especially as it relates to your efforts in the everyday world. It means that the Prayers of others must become important to you in any and every arena.

Agreement with others in Prayer unlocks dimensions not accessible any other way.

Sometimes you'll have to delay key decisions until you have direction from God. Depending on what you're doing, that can be awkward. But in the end, it's well worth it. Before you build that orphanage, plant that satellite church, buy that company, join that group, or adopt that new strategy – you'd be wise to do more than *think* twice: *pray twice*. That doesn't mean you have to go to a cabin in the woods and hold all your calls for every decision. While sometimes that is exactly what is needed, often you must navigate with your hand on the tiller, your heart engaged with His. He'll lead you in the midst of the everyday world – if you'll tune in.

Yes, you can run a 'successful' business or other initiative without Him, flying on your own Skill and Courage, inventing your own Unconventional Tactics, not inquiring of the Lord. Sometimes the world combines these three keys more effectively than Christians, and produces significant results. That kind of success, however, will not defeat real Goliaths or echo in heaven: it blooms and disappears. That's definitely not the path of a Giant Slayer. Your success, David, must be made of the right stuff, down to the core. Yet by all means, as you forge ahead in Prayer, expect significant, tangible results.

On the opposite extreme, there are some people who pray about everything, but do next to nothing, and produce very little. I'd call them 'hyper-spiritual'. A Giant Slayer cannot afford to pray about the same things over and over, without also being willing to act once direction comes.

Some matters are best handled in Prayer, rather than broadcast publicly. And no matter what you are trying to accomplish, everything has a spiritual side. So if you want to experience the full

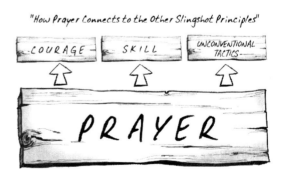

"How Prayer Connects to the Other Slingshot Principles"

COURAGE → SKILL → UNCONVENTIONAL TACTICS

PRAYER

measure of victory possible in your endeavors, you must be sure to displace unseen limiting factors, while also dealing appropriately with seen ones.

Here's one word of caution before we move on: *Be aware of doing all the talking.* Prayer can quickly become a fruitless religious exercise when you fill the air with words without pause. It's not the many words you say: it's the *interaction* with your Heavenly Father. Again I say, LISTEN.

Prayer is so crucial that entire books have been written about it, but what you need to carry away from this section is that Prayer holds special status among these four keys. It's no coincidence that the Slingshot Principles are numbered, and that Prayer appears first on the list. When properly embraced, it is a supernatural gateway that profoundly elevates the effectiveness of the other keys, and it brings a sense of fulfillment that is unparalleled.

God is eager to speak with you, David!

Key of PRAYER – Section Notes

- *Fervent Prayer connects you with God and **attracts His strength**.*

- The more you communicate with God through Prayer; the more you begin to care about the things He cares about. This progressive, internal change **radically increases** your potential.

- *Agreement with others in Prayer unlocks dimensions not accessible any other way.*

- *Make sure to **listen when praying**, as well as talk.*

- *Prayer holds **special status** among the four keys because it touches all the others, invites the work of the Supremely Able Helper, and acts as the **greatest force multiplier**.*

#2: The Key of COURAGE

"The wicked run away when no one is chasing them, but the godly are as bold as lions." *Prov. 28:1 NLT*

COURAGE ACTS BOLDLY, STEPPING UP AND PUTTING FAITH INTO MOTION.

A comrade is critically wounded on the battlefield, but despite the deadly crossfire screaming overhead, you go back to rescue him. Facing overwhelming odds and tremendous risk of failure, you launch out to fulfill an Inspired Dream. You step up to a real Giant and look him in the eyes, without backing down. Each of these things is only possible with the Key of Courage.

This key is usually in plain sight and available to everyone, yet surprisingly few pick it up. <u>Many think it belongs to someone else</u>. Unlike Faith, which reaches out to <u>believe</u> an answer before it can be seen with human eyes - *Courage must often <u>act</u> before being certain of the outcome.* And this is one of its most powerful and important qualities.

David, there are many times in life where important things hang in the balance and you need to act, despite not being *sure* of what will happen. This does not mean you are not a person of Faith. In those moments, you must summon Courage. Just remember this: **where no risk is present, no Courage is required**. So decide now to not let the appearance of risk immediately throw you, since facing it helps you call upon this potent ally. And given that you need to use all four Slingshot Principles together to experience maximum effect, said another way: if you aren't able, or willing, to employ Courage to face real risk - you will slay no Giants.

Do you remember the story of Esther? Hers is a stunning example of Courage at work.

Esther's Courage

A powerful king named Xerxes once was married to a queen who publicly insulted him without apology. As a result of her defiance, the King banished her; he then began a search far and wide to find a replacement queen.

In the process he discovered a beautiful Israelite girl named Esther. The King took special interest in her, yet never knew her ethnic background, because her wise uncle had instructed her not to tell anyone. Eventually, the King chose Esther to be his Queen.

Sometime later, an evil man named Haman found favor with King Xerxes and was promoted to the head of the government. This man hated Esther's uncle and all his people, the Israelites, so he devised a wicked plan to have them all murdered and all their wealth plundered. Not knowing his own queen was in danger, the King went along with the plan to annihilate the Israelites, because Haman convinced him they were dangerous to the kingdom.

Queen Esther found out about this plot and was understandably devastated. All of her people were to be wiped out in a single day, with the preapproval of the King! And that day was fast approaching.

> *If you aren't able, or willing, to employ Courage to face real risk - you will slay no Giants.*

What should she do? Hide and not reveal her identity? Maybe she could at least save herself. What made matters worse is that Queen Esther hadn't been invited to speak with the King in almost a month. And the law said that anyone appearing before the king uninvited would be put to death - unless the king decided, on the spur of the moment, to grant them permission. Now that's a pretty scary situation, I think you'll agree!

Even so, Esther decided to risk her own life on behalf of her people. Here is the message she sent to her uncle, to relay to all the Jews in the capital city:

> "…Fast for me. Don't eat or drink for three days, either day or night. I and my maids will fast with you. If you will do this, I'll go to the king, even though it's forbidden. If I die, I die." *Est. 4:16 MSG*

David, focus on that last statement: "If I die, I die." Queen Esther took the most informed plan of action she had, *yet was unsure whether those steps would result in her success – or her death.* The outcome hung in the balance and the danger was real, but she took bold action anyway. She was a person of Faith, yet uncertain of the consequences of her actions. The story doesn't say that three angels appeared to her and said, "Don't worry, if you'll do this, we'll save everyone including you." Instead, she had to trust God and summon her Courage.

It's the turning point in the story. Esther goes on to find favor with the King, shrewdly exposes Haman, and the Lord works through her to overthrow the plot against her people. Yet without a girl willing to step up *in spite of* tremendous risk, what would have happened?

Remember what Shadrach, Meshach and Abednego said as they faced the fiery furnace?

> "Nebuchadnezzar, we do not need to defend ourselves before you. If we are thrown into the blazing furnace, the God whom we serve is able to save us. He will rescue us from your power, Your Majesty. But even if he doesn't, we want to make it clear to you, Your Majesty, that we will never serve your gods or worship the gold statue you have set up." *Dan. 3:16-18 NLT*

Once again, you can see an element of danger and uncertainty that did not stop Courage; you can see Courage at work right alongside Faith. What an incredible duo!

A Truth Often Missed

Faith may inform Courage and even work together with it, but does NOT replace it.

Before we continue, let me tell you why all this matters so much. I'm not doing this to split hairs over words; the goal is far greater than that. It truly makes a difference: it's for you to grow in Courage so dramatically that your life changes. Because when you grab hold of the Key of Courage, David, your life will change. As you learn to unlock doors with this key, what once seemed an unlikely turn of events will become your daily experience.

You see, when Courage and Faith are just sort of lumped together, as if they sort of do the same job, they don't serve you to nearly the extent they could; they produce far less than what is possible. But when they are BOTH present, look out! I know you already have some Faith and sincerely want to increase it: you couldn't have come this far on your journey without Faith. Yet don't you know some people who diligently study the Inspired Guidebook, and their Faith is always growing, but their lives seem to be standing still? How is this possible? What are they missing? Here is what:

Faith usually needs Courage to come into full bloom.

Picture this. You are sitting in a room where a diverse group of people are hanging out, sipping coffee, and informally talking about religion. One person mentions how all religions seem the same: people meet and learn about the God or gods they believe in, share a code of conduct or rules, and allow learned values to inform their actions.

> *Courage is often what separates those who are becoming more, from those simply dreaming about it.*

Another person chimes in that religion is the basis of many conflicts in the world. And a third person offers the idea that people are always trying to find God through religion, which never seems to work.

The thought crosses your mind that actually Christianity is quite different, because it's the only 'religion' where

God *comes to man* in human form and makes a sacrifice that brings *forgiveness* to save him. The mission is fundamentally different: God is seeking men, rather than the reverse. David, this is what you believe and it's part of your Faith.

But though you are right there with the words on the tip of your tongue, you keep quiet. Though you have Faith that what you believe is true, you either don't know how to, or you choose not to, summon the Courage to speak up. Aha, now you see it! And that small example from everyday life has broader applications. There are so many things you can do when your Faith is connected to action through Courage!

Courage is often what separates those who are becoming more, from those simply dreaming about it.

There are many, many Christians standing in Faith, David - and that is precisely the problem! They stand, but they rarely *step*. Courage steps up! Standing in Faith is certainly better than sitting, but it's not the only posture of victory. Often Courage is the big difference-maker between *having* convictions and *living* them: having convictions is

A Secret to Courage

Here is one of the most powerful ways to increase Courage.

Think about the word en-Courage. It means to boost Courage. If you can learn to listen to God not only for your own True Identity & Special Assignment but that of others, and then tell them what you hear, you can deliver remarkable encouragement. Such divine [inspired] insight goes straight past defenses and directly to the heart, stirring Courage deep within.

essential, acting on them is even better. Even when great things are ultimately achieved by Faith, it is Courage that takes the actual step. It takes Courage to actually lift your foot, step out of the boat, and step onto the water.

How Courage Acts & Other Qualities

Now think about this. *Courage acts in spite of fear.* Most people freeze up when they are afraid. For example, many people are afraid of Giants, which is why they stand around waiting for a champion like you to step up. Yet Courage is not saying to yourself: "I'm not afraid. I'm not afraid. I'm not afraid." Courage is acting anyway.

You'll also find that sometimes your Courage must act more quickly than your Faith is ready to; a situation may demand it. Yet Courage is not foolhardy or presumptuous. It can turn the tide and save the day, whether on the battlefield or in the everyday world. Without Courage, many opportunities are lost by default.

Yet the Key of Courage is not simply for yourself, David: you need to value Courage, notice it, and EN-courage others too. Reward their acts of Courage. When Courage runs through a group, great things are always just a step away.

Courage is contagious.

One of the best ways to spread Courage is to increase your own. When you stand beside someone who steps out boldly despite adversity and risk, do you notice that something inside you begins to rise up, making you believe that you can step out too? That's Courage. *And this mysterious way it travels between people makes it unique among the four keys;* this is important to note for future achievements. Like many things, Courage can also be developed. As you win smaller victories along the way and see how God delivers you through them, your Courage will grow.

For many Kingdom citizens, lack of Courage is what limits them more than anything else.

Time and again I encounter people who quit too early, or who backed down when it was time to step up. It often turns out *not* that they weren't persistent, or a person of Faith, but that they lacked the Courage to keep going. A small amount of encouragement could have made the difference, but it was nowhere to be found. I wonder if God sent a message to encourage them and they didn't listen, or maybe the person who was meant to pass it along never spoke up. The ability to encourage others is sometimes viewed as not very important, but in this world of doubt, fear, and discouragement, it is actually a vital and powerful skill: one you should develop, David.

David, this whole process can snowball in either direction. As you step out in Courage and victories result, as you weather some storms and keep moving forward, Courage grows.

As Courage grows, your life makes more of an impact.

Unfortunately, the more you back down from opportunities, the reverse is also true. Do not allow failures or setbacks to sap your Courage from future moments when you must step up. Giants will try to get you to think this way; instead, treat setbacks as part of your growth process. Without Courage, life not only stinks - it *shrinks*.

Courage is deeper than confidence, and is required to accomplish great things in the everyday world. When you want to drive Giants from the land God has promised you, you have to summon Courage: there are no substitutes. Develop yours by consistently taking bold action when you know you should, and asking God for more. Also, continue to gather clarity about your True Identity and Special Assignment: moving along the road of Destiny bolsters Courage.

Remember, David, when it's time, and whether or not anyone else will – dare to step out and take a stand.

#3: The Key of SKILL

"Do you see a man skillful in his work? He will stand before kings; he will not stand before obscure men." *Prov. 22:29 ESV*

SKILL PROPELS AND ADVANCES YOU (AND YOUR SMOOTH STONE) TOWARD YOUR INTENDED TARGET.

To defeat Goliaths, David, you need the Key of Skill. It helps you sling a Smooth Stone on target, and it's also crucial to create advancement in life. The great news is that each of us has access to the Key of Skill, because each of us has been given Skills we may develop! Sadly though, often due to misunderstanding the role of Skill or discounting its use, many Kingdom citizens fail to employ this Key appropriately, resulting in parts of Destiny remaining unfulfilled. In other words, David, they *assume* (because God is with them) that they needn't ever bother to diligently apply themselves in matters of the everyday world, calling all such efforts "striving".

But even when God brings stunning supernatural power into a situation, He often uses skilled, obedient people in the process. Remember the story of Daniel and his friends being "10 times <u>more qualified</u>" than others, as a result of God's hand on their lives? (Dan 1:20) Rather than telling Daniel "Don't bother studying or applying yourself at all, because I couldn't care less about Skill," *God instead multiplied their <u>natural</u> wisdom and understanding, <u>as they applied themselves</u>.* Rather than <u>avoiding</u> Skill development, God amplified it! This is a stunning example of how He can also work through your Skill, David.

While it's a huge mistake to rely on Skill <u>by itself</u> (since that may indeed lead to ungodly pride, thinking you are a 'self-made man'), **when used in conjunction with the other Slingshot Principles, Skill produces great effect for Kingdom citizens.**

Becoming Skilled does not mean you are stealing some of God's glory, David, or that your efforts will simply be an 'act of the flesh'. *That only happens when you unwisely take complete credit for the results, or when your motives or mission are contrary to God's.* To avoid that trap, do what Daniel did: allow the Supremely Able Helper to guide you in becoming more Skillful. *As you diligently apply yourself to whatever task God has given you to do,* instead of simply trying to develop Skill through human strength and wisdom, *ask and believe Him to direct and multiply your efforts,* just as He did for Daniel. You will be amazed at how He will answer that prayer, and as only He can do!

The Often-Underestimated Importance of Skill Development

Skill is critical to advancement ("standing before kings"), and pursuing Skill does <u>not</u> mean that a person is not also dependent on God. Using your Skill should be *a glorious expression of Faith,* just as it was for Daniel and for your ancient ancestor David: Faith that, *with God's help,* you can indeed step up and defeat Goliath, using Skills that God has given you.

Unfortunately, the bone-grinding, sometimes mind-numbing repetition of the Skill development process to mastery level is something many would-be Giant Slayers ignore or try to shortcut. That is a grave mistake. Without Skill, you are under-equipped for your Special Assignment.

Not everything from God comes with 'no assembly required'. Like many things He provides, your skills start like seeds, so cultivate them as an act of Faith. Without the Key of Skill, you'll often lose battles: don't presume you will win simply because you are God's child. Trusting the Supremely Able Helper to help you be prepared, and to guide your preparation and decisions is one thing – and it's essential. But presumption – <u>simply assuming that God will make particular situations turn out a certain way,</u> even if you haven't done *your* due diligence – is not only extremely foolish, but it's a sin; in effect, you would be demanding that God jump up and *serve you*, whenever and however you tell Him to.

Whether you are a teacher, potter, pastor, entrepreneur, scientist, manager, or attorney - **do whatever it takes to master your craft,** and learn to enjoy the process of skill development. More schooling, or spending time with an expert or mentor, could be exactly what you need. If God has called you to Government or Missions work or to lead an alternative band, seek to develop exceptional Skill in that area. If you manage the bank or design clothes, do it 'as unto the Lord'. Seek opportunities for Skill development. Don't fall for the idea that 'Skill is not important to achievement as a Kingdom citizen, because God just prefers to magically make everything happen.' He can, of course - but usually He doesn't.

Ask God to help you develop your skills, David; He *wants* to help you with this – and He knows exactly what help you need. When you proceed in the direction of your Special Assignment, you'll find that skill development comes more naturally, though not necessarily easily. Hang in there; don't stop short of the goal. God wants you to be able to stand before kings, but as the Inspired Guidebook says, you need to be skilled to do that.

You are an instrument in God's hand. He loves displaying the skills and talents He created in you and accomplishing great things with you! In fact, did you know that the very first time the Inspired Guidebook uses the phrase "filled with the Spirit of God", it is used in conjunction with Skill!

> "See, I have called by name Bezalel the son of Uri, the son of Hur, of the tribe of Judah: and I have filled him with the Spirit of God, in wisdom, and in understanding, and in knowledge, and in all manner of workmanship, to devise skilful works, to work in gold, and in silver, and in brass, and in cutting of stones for setting, and in carving of wood, to work in all manner of workmanship." *Ex 31:2-5 ASV*

When Bezalel was "filled with the Spirit", the result was a great demonstration of Skill. Isn't that interesting?!! You see, David, so often the Supremely Able Helper uses and works through your human Skills. So work *with* Him to hone yours, and give Him the glory as you advance.

A Coffee Roaster Who Valued Skill

As with the Key of Prayer, while your Skill set as an individual is tremendously important, using the Key of Skill to full extent is bigger than one person. To fully turn this key - and not only slay a Goliath, but go on to do even greater things, David - you will have to place a higher value on not just your personal Skills, but the skills of others too.

Let's imagine you're an entrepreneur with an Inspired Idea to import, roast, and wholesale coffee in your region - and also open a retail coffee shop/café. What might it look like to use the Key of Skill as you get started?

Let's say that in addition to the basic idea, one of the passions which fuel this mission is a Vision to support orphanage construction in Africa (where you also have a contact to source beans). You plan to donate a portion of proceeds, visit and help, and also purchase coffee from those who will contribute to the effort in Africa.

Back home, you want your coffee shop to have a cool vibe. So you get together with your would-be partner and start discussing the possibilities. You begin to explore what it will take to launch, you visit possible locations, research the competition, and talk to another person you know who works with coffee. The amount of information available online is overwhelming, but you find some interesting and useful stuff. You buy a helpful book, specifically about this niche, which has some great tips. You share the idea with family, friends, and your small group leader. You seek out input from qualified sources on as many aspects of the business as you can.

Your partner has a good bit of experience in another industry and a solid head for business; she even invested in a small business or two before. You meet together for a month to strategize, and you write an executive summary and a business plan; you avoid shortcuts, lazy calculations without details, and really think it through. You determine the best legal structure. You and your partner make an ironclad commitment that whatever happens, you will give it your best effort for at least 18 months, no giving up or backing out.

You realize that many 'Christian' businesses (and others too) fail, not for lack of Vision, but lack of Skill, so you are determined to have exceptional quality product, well-trained staff, and great execution in all areas of the business, including Leadership, Management, Sales & Marketing, Customer Service, Accounting, etc... You identify potential weaknesses and strengths, and strategies to deal with both. You go ahead and do the things you don't feel like doing or that you may not be as strong in, simply because you have determined these must be done with Skill, rather than half-baked.

Because you have a limited budget, you can't afford the best of everything right off the bat, so to compensate for this you make every effort to make shrewd investments. You prioritize which things must be handled by experts, such as your electrical work and roaster setup. Things you do yourself behind the scenes, you do with excellence; in some areas this takes a little extra time because you're not a true expert, but you do your best. When the resulting level is not acceptable, you have someone else help you redo it, creatively working strategic trade-outs with people you know.

Since you have chosen to value Skill, you decide not to settle for the cheap pastries that are all around town. You effectively negotiate a special deal with a relatively unknown local bakery that has outstanding product, thus creating a win-win. You use skilled contractors on your build out, find some exceptional local artists to display artwork, and hire a web company proven to produce high-quality websites. (Of course you are praying and looking for the guidance of the Supremely Able Helper every step of the way.) You test different beans and roasting methods to find the best flavors and most cost-effective delivery. You commission a local potter, who is an exceptional craftsperson, to make mugs for sale.

Many 'Christian' businesses (and others too) fail, not for lack of Vision, but lack of Skill.

You choose the right lighting, and bring in a friend who is an interior designer to help create the right vibe.

And that's just the beginning: you continue like this in every aspect of your launch and management of the operation. Do you get the picture, David? Valuing Skill affects the way you do everything – and it should. The Key of Skill is a mentality, not just a personal bag of tricks.

Giant Slayers who go on to do great things value Skill. They develop their own Skills, recognize Skill in others, sense where Skill is lacking, attract those who have needed Skill, and develop Skill where needed.

Why are there problems with the coffee and customer complaints on Tuesday mornings? Has the employee working that day been trained properly? Sure, that person is likable, can quote many passages from the Inspired Guidebook and was in a tight spot when you hired him, but how are his Skills coming along? He might need extra training or coaching. Why do you keep getting such great comments about that one barista? Likely she is skilled in dealing with people, and pays attention to detail while preparing their coffee.

Giant Slayers who go on to do great things value Skill. They develop their own Skills, recognize Skill in others, sense where Skill is lacking, attract those who have needed Skill, and develop it where needed.

When Skill Is Missing

It's a grave error when some of the Kingdom family hears that the overall battle is the Lord's, so they mistakenly conclude that He will completely solve every problem directly from heaven, with or without using people: as if no one needs to actually get involved or become skilled enough to lead. Of course God can do anything He wants any way He wants, but - as the Inspired Guidebook makes clear right from the beginning - so often He chooses to use <u>people</u>, David, to accomplish His purposes. And He deliberately gave you your different skills to help you achieve the goals and purposes He wants you to achieve.

It's too often the case that people blame God for a failure which is actually their own: the failure to develop needed Skill. I have observed firsthand, time and again, leaders and organizations unable, or even unwilling, to value Skill in an area which ultimately ended up sidetracking what was a wonderful, inspired plan. Often the leader saw the value of Skill in areas where they personally possessed it, and even other areas they deemed important, but missed it in one or two places that ended up costing them. So when attempting something, David, surround yourself not simply with like-minded people, but *also* those with complementary Skill. (And listen to them.)

Don't rely on Skill alone, of course, but look to raise the level of Skill in the mix of what you're doing. Those who foolishly rely on Skill alone, as if talent by itself makes the world go round, are making a serious mistake. Besides, victories won on talent alone tend to be short-lived and to celebrate only the victor; you are aiming higher than that, David.

The result of Kingdom citizens devaluing Skill is a world where strategic places of leadership and influence are largely dominated by those who don't know God, yet who possess more Skill to lead. And then those leadership positions in government, media, business, and education – places of huge strategic influence and power over people's lives - are much more vulnerable to being overrun by Giants. (Remember my parking lot experience?) So when Kingdom citizens in these arenas are out-managed, out-thought, and out-done by those who develop and use their God-given Skill better than we do, it is not simply a personal tragedy, it can truly be a tragedy of monumental proportions.

A Word of Advice: Never Underestimate a Giant

Giants are thrilled when you undervalue Skill, David. They prefer that you do so, because then they enjoy a strategic advantage over you. It's easy to underestimate how skilled a Giant is, but avoid that common mistake. A Giant is a dominant force for a reason; he has defeated many Challengers along the way. The Giant may be ungodly, but he is a Skilled Champion just the same.

And also remember that the "right kind" of champions are made in the off-season. **When you're standing face to face with Goliath, you don't need more practice: by then it's too late. You need to have *already practiced, so put your time in ahead of time.*** Working to improve yourself behind the scenes, when not a soul is paying attention, is not always easy or fun. But sharp Skills will eventually open doors for you, David. They will help you defeat Goliath, and they will allow you to stand before kings.

Mistaken Ideas about Skill

It is a strange and unfortunate fact that *many Kingdom citizens have simply been talked out of using their God-given Skill properly, or to its full extent.* Unlike Daniel, they are listening to the wrong advice. Not surprisingly, this often leads to their defeat by Goliath: a great tragedy.

The result of Kingdom citizens devaluing Skill is a world where strategic places of leadership and influence are largely dominated by those who don't know God, yet who possess more Skill to lead.

What I want you to understand and take to heart, David, is this: as a Kingdom citizen, a desire to operate with mastery in your Special Assignment should come naturally to you. In using Skill, you are not trying to impress God, and He is not expecting you to achieve everything by your own efforts. You should use Skill because God Himself doesn't do anything half-baked, and because Skill opens certain doors not accessible through other means. So make sure you put Skill to work, and don't simply presume that in every case Faith is a replacement for lack of Skill, or *vice versa*; your Faith and your Skill need to work together.

The secret to properly using the Key of Skill, David, is to listen to the Supremely Able Helper, and seek to combine Skill with the other Slingshot Principles.

Key of SKILL – Section Notes

* *Skill **propels and advances** you toward your intended target.*

* *Skill is **crucial to create progress** in life and to fulfill your Special Assignment.*

* *Without the Key of Skill, you'll often lose battles – even **when you are God's kid.***

* *When attempting something, surround yourself not simply with like-minded people, but also those with **complementary Skill**.*

* *Giant Slayers who go on to do great things **value Skill**. They develop theirs, recognize it in others, sense where Skill is lacking, attract those who have needed Skills, and develop it where needed.*

* *Work now to **develop your Skill behind the scenes**, so you'll be ready to defeat a Giant when the time comes.*

* ***Combine Skill with the other Slingshot Principles.***

#4: The Key of UNCONVENTIONAL TACTICS

> "After all, he's famous for great and unexpected acts; there's no end to his surprises." *Job 5:9 MSG*

WELL-CHOSEN UNCONVENTIONAL TACTICS CREATE A STRATEGIC ADVANTAGE THAT OFTEN LEADS TO VICTORY.

David, your Partner is the Chief Creative Genius, the World's Leading Pioneer, and the Master of the Unexpected. He is full of innovative ideas and is not bound by what others believe is 'normal'. He is the Ultimate Thought Leader. Yet in His never-ending supply of 'fresh', He is not erratic or flighty. He builds line upon line and precept upon precept, and is the same yesterday, today, and forever. But within that framework, He can call forth unlimited creative power on a moment's notice: power that changes a person, a group, organization, region, a nation - or even rocks the entire world.

No problem you will ever face is unsolvable by God; they don't even worry Him.

God can override natural laws without breaking a sweat, or He can work within them in ways that a hundred generations of human beings would never think of. His works are marvelous and incredible. In some ways, He is anything but predictable. Strangely though, in many places that supposedly know a lot about God and claim His involvement, things seldom change.

But can any of this help *you* slay the Giant in front of you? Certainly; read on. Quite simply, the Key of Unconventional Tactics, used in Partnership with God and along with the other Slingshot Principles, can produce stunning results. This key is often the deciding factor between success and failure.

Yet for something so precious, too few Christians distinguish its value or its whereabouts. Even you may have passed right by this key. Once you are fortunate enough to pick it up and have it in your hand, though, you can't rush it or force it. It's not a 'get rich quick' scheme, nor a Giant Slayer's shortcut, nor simply 'guerilla marketing'; it's more. To be unconventional means different than expected: outside the norm.

"But unexpected by whom? What norm?"

Good question. To illustrate this, using Unconventional Tactics you might surprise a Giant, a group of people, or even a rival organization. In each case, someone has an expectation of you that causes them to underestimate you, because they expect you to act a certain way. Throughout military history, for example, it has often been the surprise attack or unconventional tactic that changed an outcome. When American soldiers in the Revolutionary War began to use natural cover, instead of standing in the open as had been the norm for generations, the war began to shift.

The Unconventional Tactic is a difference maker.

A Gaming Lesson

You are probably aware of the Wii electronic game console, created by Nintendo. Before the release of the Wii, it appeared quite possible that the once leading game giant would be ousted from the huge home gaming market by the Sony Playstation and Microsoft's XBOX 360. Facing increasingly difficult odds, why did Nintendo choose to depart from the precedent set by its rivals toward faster processors and flashier graphics? Both rivals were spending more and more resources on those goals.

But Nintendo decided to take an unconventional approach: focus on the controller experience instead - and go after new markets. Nintendo created a revolutionary interactive gaming experience which incorporated motion in new ways, so kids to parents to grandparents could all join in. Over 86 million units later, the tactics proved so revolutionary that the Wii rocketed Nintendo right back to the top of the home gaming world.

How did this happen?

Here is what Nintendo's then-president Satoru Iwata said: "With the final model of Wii in front of me, I cannot help but think, *this could not have been accomplished if we had tried to make a new game console in the conventional manner.*"

You see, David, well-chosen Unconventional Tactics are surprisingly powerful.

While it's true that God can easily beat any opposing force at its own game, such as calling down greater fire to beat fire, quite often He chooses to do things differently – *unconventionally* - using an added element of surprise. You need to know that about Him, because if He uses unexpected means at times, so should you.

Tactics are Keys to Greater Victory

A Tactic, unlike a Vision or overall Strategy, is a more specific action or clear set of actions intended to bring about a certain result. Tactics are often included in effective Plans and Visions, because a tactic is the *method* by which you intend to make the vision become a reality. For example, one organization may have a Vision to become a leading natural health and supplement store in the area. Perhaps the company has been in business for a while and hasn't yet seen the Vision unfold as they hoped. Its owners may set Objectives to increase sales, increase profitability, and stabilize cash flow as part of a plan to realize the Vision. Both the Vision and Objectives may be great, but without Tactics, such as a daily up-selling strategy, enhanced merchandizing that improves dollar yield per square foot, or a new unconventional e-marketing approach - forget it.

Larger goals are often reached through daily wins and losses at the tactical level.

David, in many engagements with people and organizations trying to create growth, I have noticed something strange. While some already had impressive, well-thought-out Vision and Strategy, some didn't. Yet *most* lacked a full complement of inspired, Unconventional Tactics and the ability to execute them.

Many times it's not the larger, over-arching Vision that determines success: it's the daily, weekly, and monthly approach to selecting and executing Tactics. It's choosing that provocative tagline in your branding that differentiates you and purposefully attracts new markets. It's meeting with that certain person because you feel inspired to do so, even though you aren't sure how they can help…or attacking a Giant with an unexpected weapon in your hand.

Strategy/Vision	Tactic
• Direction-setting, overarching • Bigger picture, more general	• Specific action or clear set of actions to bring about a desired result • Larger goals are often reached through daily wins and losses at the tactical level

Your ancient ancestor, also named David, defeated the original Goliath with Unconventional Tactics. That David (1) avoided wearing conventional armor that he wasn't used to, (2) instead of being intimidated, defiantly boasted that the Lord would give him victory, (3) *ran* to the battle line - surprising the Giant with boldness and cutting down his time to react, and (4) carried an unconventional weapon into the fight: a weapon that seemed totally weak and outmatched by Goliath's huge sword.

Do you see what I'm getting at? Many key battles are won and lost because of the Tactics chosen. Yet the secret to the Key of Unconventional Tactics is not in being different just to be different. We are talking about the kind of Tactics that are part of important, strategic concerns, not minor things such as whether to wear green socks or blue tomorrow.

It's in being different *for a reason*; *strategically* different. This may mean (1) challenging the status quo, (2) choosing the right mix of tactics to defeat a Giant, or (3) obeying particular directions from God which run counter to human logic.

Finding the best tactic requires being in touch with God and allowing Him to help you choose from among many possible courses of action.

Unusual Inspirations

Let's explore that last area for a second: *obeying clear directions from God that run counter to human logic*. Think about what happened immediately <u>before</u> certain amazing miracles that are recorded in the Inspired Guidebook:

- Snakes are on the loose among the people: all who are bitten quickly die. A man is instructed to *make a bronze snake and put it on a pole;* anyone bitten who then *looks at the bronze snake,* now survives.

- 12 representatives from the tribes of Israel are instructed to step into an overflowing river with the Ark of the Covenant. As their feet step into the water, the river parts - and the people cross on dry land.

- Men are instructed to march around a city once for six days, then on the seventh day march around it seven times and then blow trumpets and shout. The walls of the city fall to the ground.

- A woman on the verge of starvation is instructed to take her *last* morsel of flour and oil, use part *to make a cake to feed someone else,* and only then use the remainder for her and her son. The supply of flour and oil miraculously feeds them for many days, though the last bit was used up.

- Fishermen can't catch a thing after trying all night long. They are instructed to put their nets in again *into the same waters:* this time they catch so many fish the nets are breaking.

- A man spits in the dirt, makes clay of the spittle, puts it on a blind man's eyes and instructs him to go wash it off. The blind man washes it off and can immediately see.

As you know, the Inspired Guidebook is filled with many more such examples. But I want you to see that each of these accounts has something in common: directly preceding an incredible outcome were specific actions that seemed completely contrary to logic.

It's rare to receive orders like those listed above, but it's always possible, so be alert. When a moment like that comes, a lot may be riding on it, and you might not have a second chance. My point is, **there are times when, to enter into something God wants to bring about, you must absolutely obey His specific instructions which may be unconventional.**

Am I seriously saying that, to help you relocate your business, the Lord will likely direct you to walk around a building three times rather than make an offer to the owner? Not necessarily. Yet as crazy as it sounds, completely 'illogical' directions sometimes come from God. That's why you need to be aware of this possibility - and you need to know His voice! (On the other hand, this does not mean that every off-the-wall idea you have is from God.) By observing how He chooses to act in the examples we looked at, we learn something about the way He sometimes does things: *Unconventionally*. Let that word sink in.

Choosing the Right Tactics

Listen closely, David. This is where you take the talents, skills, and creativity that God has given you, and combine them with His leadings and inspiration. Yes, you team up with God!

Big problems can often be solved with inspired, well-chosen, Unconventional Tactics. If God simply wanted to bark instructions at every turn, as if you were a puppet on a string, He could do so. But in His limitless creativity, He instead made you in His image and invested you with self-awareness and self-will. He also gave you a Supremely Able Helper and put some marvelous abilities in *you*. This is a truly potent combination.

You have the ability to come up with great ideas and imaginative, Unconventional Tactics. This isn't an accident, or something you are required to turn off to be a proper Kingdom citizen. Use these gifts to the full, David.

Now imagine yourself leading a moderately successful organization that is trying to gain new market share, so you assemble a few top leaders to brainstorm. You get out the whiteboards and use as best you know how the imagination, knowledge, and talents which the Lord gave each of you. This is the wisest, most Skilled team you can put together for this effort. You incorporate excellent planning practices and come up with a lot of ideas - *but you don't stop there.*

When you have God's resources available, yet instead choose to rely completely on your own ideas and strength, it greatly reduces your odds of true success.

Your edge comes by being aware of God's presence and leading, even while you work: combine tactical planning with Prayer. If you can't pray with others, you can do one of two things. Instead of forcing a decision at the meeting, take all the best ideas home with you and pray through them that night. Allow God to shed light on which of the Tactics you should choose, or even let Him make a new suggestion to run by the team the next day. Or, if quicker action is required, you *may* simply have to stay tuned-in to the Supremely Able Helper and guide the discussion according to the leading of the Lord, right there on the spot. Either approach is far better than total reliance on human ability.

The best Unconventional Tactics are usually those informed by Prayer. This is where *innovative* plans can become not only unconventional, but *inspired.* And you often need Inspired Unconventional Tactics, so ask God to show you specific Unconventional Tactics that will lead your initiative to success.

Guerilla marketing is successful because it taps into one of God's principles; He is often surprising and does the unexpected to bring victory through unlikely heroes. After all, the unexpected and unconventional is God's idea in the first place. (Think about it.)

Here's a question: Are many Kingdom citizens known for setting trends through innovative thinking, or do we mostly blend in with the crowd? By nature, we should be pioneers, innovators, and refreshingly Unconventional, just like our Partner.

Battle Note

Your Partner is far superior to Giants and has many ways to attack and defeat them. (He is, of course, capable of superior achievement in any and every realm of the world.) Giants, on the other hand, have only certain things they are good at. Because of this, if you happen to cross one, he'll want to lure you into fighting the way he is used to. Don't! The Giant knows how to win when fighting his way. Instead, fight on your terms through the use of inspired, Unconventional Tactics.

This is one of the greatest lessons of the Slingshot.

What is available to you with God as your Partner, David, is far greater than what any Giant is capable of. That is why you must resist the urge to limit yourself to playing the game as the Giant wants to play it. On your side you have Heaven's possibilities, accessible anytime. On the Giant's side is intimidation, some power, and only limited skills.

Key of UNCONVENTIONAL TACTICS
Section Notes

- *Unconventional Tactics **often make the difference** between success and failure.*

- *Larger goals are often reached through **daily wins and losses** at the tactical level.*

- *The secret to using Unconventional Tactics is not in being different simply to be different. It's in being different for a reason: **strategically different**.*

- ***Big problems can often be solved** with inspired, well-chosen, Unconventional Tactics.*

- *The use of Unconventional Tactics **does not negate the need for Conventional Tactics** in many other areas.*

- *The best Unconventional Tactics are quite often **informed by Prayer**.*

The Slingshot Principles at Work

What's so special about the combination of Prayer, Courage, Skill, and Unconventional Tactics? While the previous pages bring to light a few key points, there is more to explore.

What about Vision, Worship, Favor, Character, Discipline, Leadership, Teamwork, and so many other important factors? David, it's not that you won't incorporate other things you've learned along the way. But frankly, numerous volumes have been written on those topics, yet most people are still searching for breakthrough after reading them. Try using the Slingshot Principles, without neglecting the others.

Let me leave you with a better idea of how this combination came into this book. After the Lord highlighted it for me, I was not allowed to change it, despite many attempts. After wrestling with dozens of other possibilities, I felt a little silly when it finally hit me that I wasn't to alter the original four. In the end, it's these four that hold something particularly powerful when used together. *Though I don't profess to understand the synergy fully, I am persuaded that used properly, the Slingshot Principles will create significant advance in your life.*

Of course in some cases, David, you may find yourself facing a specific obstacle that will yield to a certain sub-combination. Say for example you're trying to write an effective executive summary to raise interest in a project (Skill) for a business you feel inspired to start, but it's not working. So instead of giving up, you pray more diligently and purposefully (Prayer), and it comes to your attention that there are three areas you should highlight in the summary that don't come through well enough yet. You rewrite it, and interest rises immediately.

Or perhaps you're trying to grow a non-profit organization and you have hit a wall. You've prayed and done all you know to do, but nothing is changing. You go back to the Lord and ask specifically about what tactics to use (Unconventional Tactics), and also invest time improving the way you are communicating with donors (Skill). You step up and contact a few new potential donors who you once felt a little intimidated by but now feel inspired to contact (Courage).

The Lord impresses you with an innovative way to highlight another good cause as part of your effort (Unconventional Tactics), which seems crazy, but you do it. You also realize that one of your people simply lacks the skills you need for what you are doing (Skill), so you reposition that person (Courage) and hire an outside freelancer. Remarkably, new opportunities and traction arrive soon after.

Or, let's say you can't find the job you want, and times are tough. You know God has promised you more, but you just don't see it. You have already prayed (Prayer) but nothing is happening. A friend mentions that your resume looks just like everyone else's. Another person tells you about a job opportunity you feel under-qualified for but think you can probably do; yet it may be over your head, so you've been hesitant to go apply for it. You seek out a more striking layout for your resume (Unconventional Tactics, Skill), make contact on the job (Courage), and, surprisingly, the firm really loves your resume and you end up getting the job. (Sometimes combining the Slingshot Principles attracts other potent allies, such as Favor.)

That's a quick look at the Slingshot Principles in practical action in the everyday world. You'll probably find many different ways to combine them. That's great; use them to the full. Though they are useful in almost anything you do, they are especially helpful in pioneering and launching projects, or when you need to *propel* something. And most of all, they will help you defeat Goliaths.

The Secret of Conventional Tactics

A strategic emphasis on Unconventional Tactics does NOT negate the need for Conventional ones. You need both. Skillful management, for example, requires mastering a number of sound, conventional Tactics in addition to other unconventional ones you might employ at times. Don't make the mistake of trying to become so unconventional in everything all the time that you end up being just plain weird.

Chapter 9

Key Takeaways & Giant Slayer Tips

- Properly applied, the Secrets of the Slingshot **give Kingdom citizens an edge** in virtually anything.

- There is **special hidden power** in uniting spiritual and physical force.

- The 4 main keys are: 1. **Prayer** 2. **Courage** 3. **Skill** 4. **Unconventional Tactics**

- Combination Factor: **The deepest secret** is not in any one of the four Keys by itself - it's in **how you use them together**.

- The Secrets of the Slingshot are especially useful in **pioneering, launching,** and **propelling**.

Chapter 10
Choosing Smooth Stones

"Then David took his shepherd's staff, selected five smooth stones from the brook, and put them in the pocket of his shepherd's pack, and with his sling in his hand approached Goliath." *1 Sam. 17:40 MSG*

You are already making excellent progress, David. Slingshot practice isn't easy, that's for sure, but the results can produce great things. Soon, Giants will fall. That is, *if* you can find the right Smooth Stones. Without Smooth Stones you won't hit the mark, no matter how good you become with a Slingshot.

I'll explain all about Smooth Stones and what they are, but before we keep going, take note. This chapter holds especially important keys, including a few which are not so obvious. *Many of these truths you have likely never heard stated like this.* I mention this because I know we are right on the brink of another rigorous climb. So if you're not quite ready to forge ahead, just rest a bit and come back later; there's no rush.

You see, those who learn *how to choose Smooth Stones* and combine that knowledge with the Slingshot Principles will enjoy an advantage in life - one available only to Kingdom citizens. When you put Smooth Stones and Slingshot Principles together - ZING! - watch what happens. That's why it would be best if you are well rested and mentally sharp before proceeding. Makes sense? Alright then, here we go.

What is A Smooth Stone?

Think of a Smooth Stone as an *inspired means* to deliver an *exceptional impact*.

A person who can pick the right Smooth Stone is a person who can recognize the right means to use in a given situation. When critical situations hang in the balance, the right Smooth Stone can be used to shift them. To do so, though, it must have certain qualities. The amazing thing is that there are Smooth Stones for every arena and situation in life, but you have to know where to look and what to look for.

The secrets of Smooth Stones are not widely known. You see, most people have been taught about Dreams, Passion, Ideas, Purpose, and Vision. All these are tremendously valuable. We need them. However, the average Western Christian could already teach a message on each of those subjects. Yet Giants are still in their face.

While almost everyone has a Dream, few have a Smooth Stone.

A Smooth Stone is an instrument that's ready for action, an Inspired Idea with substance, an actual means to do something. There's some weight to it. When you roll it around in your hand it feels right. A Smooth Stone has more shape to it than a Dream, a Passion, or an Idea. It has a distinguishable form. It's tangible. It looks more like a solution, a project, an organization, a new initiative, or even a building block. Many times, Smooth Stones are building blocks of Dreams.

Without Smooth Stones, Dreams change little. _With_ Smooth Stones, Dreams change so much.

How to Recognize Smooth Stones

Just as a gun fires bullets, a Slingshot fires stones. And some stones fly better than others.

"So where are these Smooth Stones, what do they look like, and how do I choose them?"

Excellent questions, David. Let's look at the nature of Smooth Stones so they will be easier to recognize. You should know that some will never work, while others are good but not great. Others work for you, but not for someone else. Only a few fly straight and true.

"How can you tell one from another just by looking?"

Smooth Stones come in many shapes and sizes, but their intended use is the same, to (1) *help you deliver an exceptional impact which is part of your Special Assignment, (2) displace opposing forces,* and *(3) glorify God.* Unless your Stone is headed toward all three, it's not the kind we're talking about.

"Hang on a second; time out. This reads like another riddle, but I'd say choosing Smooth Stones is a pretty important topic for Slingshots. Can you make this practical enough so I can choose wisely?"

Point well taken, David. The subject of selecting Smooth Stones is so critical to becoming a Giant Slayer that *I'm going to do my best to plainly tell you exactly what to look for and what not to.* So get ready.

The Hidden Power of Smooth Stones

Some may not understand why this next section matters so much and so be tempted to rush ahead; others will find precious keys. The choice is yours. Look carefully.

Though Smooth Stones deliver spiritual impact as well as natural effect, they <u>always</u> have physical form. That doesn't sound too earth shattering at first, does it? It's so simple, how could it be important? But it is…

"So it's a rock I can see, eh?"

Yes.

If you can't see any of it with your physical eyes, it is NOT a Smooth Stone, period. Smooth Stones are never purely unseen things. **Inspired Ideas, Dreams, and Visions by themselves, therefore, are not Smooth**

Stones. Remember that, David! That doesn't mean those aren't important or real; they're just not Smooth Stones – yet.

Think with me for a minute. Why did God *multiply* loaves and fish instead of *creating* them out of thin air - <u>choosing to create supernatural impact (bring a miraculous solution) using a combination of *physical means and spiritual ones*</u>? As part of the solution to the greatest problem mankind has ever faced - sin - why did God send His Son into the physical universe as a human, instead of solving everything in the invisible spiritual world? Why did Jesus speak of giving a thirsty person an actual glass of water (a clearly natural cause and effect), yet reveal that the same natural act was also fulfilling a spiritual reality of ministering to the Lord Himself?

I'll tell you why: because **the natural universe is connected to the spiritual universe – no matter where you go in it.** Business is not unspiritual, neither is Medicine, Government, nor Entertainment. Whether or not people choose to downplay their spiritual sides, the connection exists anyway. And herein lies one of the greatest secrets of the Giant Slayer. To defeat a Goliath, or to truly change the world according to one's Special Assignment, requires a combination of natural and spiritual actions.

"Okay, tell me again how this helps me."

Well, David, it changes many things. By understanding this principle, you develop a Giant Slayer's Mindset. No matter what they are doing, Giant Slayers pay attention to, and operate consistently in, *both* the natural and spiritual realms. They lead integrated lives: they don't go to Base Camp to do spiritual things but then spend the rest of the week thinking they can simply operate from their natural strength and wisdom. They realize that the spiritual and the natural are always intertwined.

When you and I do everything *as unto the Lord* as we are commanded, there is no such thing as a 'secular' job. Neither is it true that only pastors and missionaries have 'sacred' roles in life. In the Kingdom, we all have sacred roles. Everything we set our hand to, every person we interact with, we do as a Kingdom citizen. We are God's children 100% of the time, and Kingdom citizens as well.

On the other hand, if you believe deep down that the more spiritual you are, the less the physical realm matters, or that only a few select things in life have a spiritual side, then you will always have trouble finding the right Smooth Stones and launching them effectively. **You see, David, Smooth Stones impact life in the everyday world <u>and</u> advance the Kingdom of God**. (We could explore detailed theology about this, which might bore you to tears;[3] not now. Instead, <u>I want you to see that such beliefs produce two major groups of people, neither of them Giant Slayers</u>.)

Lopsided Stones & Two Groups of Kingdom Citizens

1) "Spiritual Things are All That Matter!"

One group of Kingdom citizens prefers to emphasize unseen things, with undersized regard for seen ones. Unfortunately, though on one level they feel great satisfaction, the full impact they are destined to bring to the everyday world rarely occurs. But since they value unseen things more anyway, they usually come to accept this way of life as normal.

Picture someone who is present at Base Camp for every special conference, prayer meeting, and Inspired Guidebook study. They regularly help out at the local food pantry on weekends and serve in children's ministry and choir. They often get praised for how 'spiritual' they are. Yet despite such worthy pursuits, while they work at their full-time job, they spend days continually wishing they were doing something more 'spiritual'. They believe that God has put it in their heart to serve on the mission field, teach, and also write children's books, but they never seem to be able to quite connect the dots to get there. Why not?

2) "I Guess I'm 'Just' a Business Person!"

The other group tends to miss the spiritual side of things in the everyday world, as if Base Camp-type things are spiritual, but the rest of life really isn't. Due to this disconnect, deep down they worry that there

3 For more on this subject refer to the Giants Workbook, available at www.tribeofgiantslayers.com

is something more meaningful they should be doing with their lives. Their achievements may be notable, but they feel hollow. This group generally misses both Partnership with God in the everyday world, and also the significance of spiritual targets they could be hitting through their daily pursuits.

Picture a Kingdom citizen who builds a successful business, but also goes to Base Camp on Sundays. They feel that 'spiritual' life only occasionally enters the rest of their week. They run their business with their own wisdom, rarely if ever seeking the Lord regarding business decisions. No real partnership with God exists; after all, it's "just work", right? This person is uncertain, though, whether they're truly fulfilling their Special Assignment and doing exactly what God is telling them to. "But hey, at least the business is going well, so I can give lots of money to Base Camp and other worthy causes, and that makes me a solid Kingdom citizen, right?" Wrong, my friend.

Strangely, both types of Kingdom citizens believe they are not experiencing all that God intended for them - and they're both right.

They both believe, wrongly, that everything that happens at Base Camp is inherently *more* spiritual, and all of life outside Base Camp is *less* so. So the first type of Kingdom citizen runs themselves ragged trying to be more 'spiritual', possibly having bouts of burnout or even depression, yet too often unable to fully achieve the inspired dream in their heart, as they are frequently limited by what appear to be 'natural' reasons such as lack of finances, poor planning, or ineffective stewardship. The second type, on the other hand, often feels like a second-class Kingdom citizen because they (wrongly) believe they weren't called to 'full-time ministry', so they miss the powerful combined natural/spiritual impact they could be making in the everyday world, right where God has placed them.

"So what does this have to do with Smooth Stones?"

Plenty. You see, David, here's what happens. Because both types of Kingdom citizen have learned to think and live life off-balance in one way or another, if they pick up any Stones at all *they tend to pick **lopsided stones**, which don't fly straight enough to slay Giants.* Due to their unbalanced perspective, stones that look smooth to these two groups won't actually do the job.

More probably, instead of picking up a stone when faced with a Goliath (provided they could summon enough Courage), the first group might keep praying, believing, and imagining what might happen if the Giant were removed, but never find the means to actually complete the job. Someone from the second group would likely just grab the currently popular conventional weapon – the latest social-networking marketing strategy, maybe - and try as best they could to beat the Giant at his own game. Each group might make some difference, but neither would slay the Giant.

Spiritual + Natural = Giant Slayer

The real solution would come when a Giant Slayer stepped up. They would carefully select some Smooth Stones that the Lord inspired them to pick, trusting that one had a divine assignment to hit the mark. The key would be not only selecting the right Stone, nor Prayer alone, though the Giant Slayer would do both. The Giant Slayer would already have honed their Skill, developed Courage, learned how to Partner with God and to use Unconventional Tactics. They would address the spiritual side of the battle by declaring that victory would come from the Lord. Then, **in a remarkable display that _combined spiritual and natural means_, the Giant Slayer would emerge victorious from the seemingly hopeless battle**.

Let's look at an example, David: think for a moment about the book you hold in your hands. This book began as an Inspired Idea and would have stayed one, had I not given it substance. At first it was hardly a Smooth Stone, but eventually it began to take shape. When it became smooth enough, I hurled it using the very same Slingshot Principles I have taught you.

I have soaked it with Prayer, stepped forward with the Courage I have, valued Skill through every part of its release, and employed Unconventional Tactics on multiple fronts. I launched it in partnership with God, and directly at an enemy that is keeping a generation of

Kingdom citizens limited to far less than what is possible. This book is part of my Special Assignment, designed to glorify God and displace opposing forces.

You see what I mean?

Dreams vs. Smooth Stones Summary

Dream	Smooth Stone
• Is often completely invisible	• Has at least some *physical* substance
• Often rough, half baked	• Is smoothed into something
• Almost everyone has at least one	• Few people have them
• Frequently never come to pass	• Actually hits the mark far more often
• Often glorify only the visionary	• Impact glorifies God

The Artist, The Contractor & The Entrepreneur

Suppose there are three people who dream about supplying fresh water to those who lack it; they each believe their desire is connected to their Special Assignment. One is an artist, one a contractor, and one an entrepreneur.

None of them have a Smooth Stone yet, so HOW will they go about making their vision a reality? (By the way, this question tends to help you find places where Smooth Stones are. *The Smooth Stone often carries the specific 'how' for a particular season or situation.*) After all, unless each of the three finds a concrete means to take action, nothing will happen; no difference will be made.

The artist has an inspired idea to create a series of paintings: each painting will illustrate compelling scenes of thirst, survival, and hidden beauty. Then he'll use the earnings to help build a well. He plans to begin work over the winter and complete the series by the following spring. As the work is completed and the project takes shape, it becomes more than an Inspired Idea - it becomes a Smooth Stone.

The contractor feels inspired to use her talents in an existing non-profit operation. So she connects with the owner and eventually begins to serve there part-time. (She is helping propel a Smooth Stone that has already been released – and, in a way, is also being like a Smooth Stone herself.)

The entrepreneur has an inspired idea to start a company that sells bottled water in the US. This enterprise will give a strategic portion of proceeds from every bottle to support the research efforts of a group developing advanced, cost-effective water filtration for tainted water sources. As the effort comes together, can you see how it resembles a Smooth Stone?

An inspired means is a Smooth Stone. It carries both unseen potential and physical impact.

One Size Does NOT Fit All, & Other Smooth Secrets

You could probably tell that the same stone would not work equally well in all three Slingshots, right? You have to find a type that works best for you and fits the situation. Yet three different Smooth Stones could all target the same Giant of unjust thirst, and hit him right between the eyes.

Just remember this - Smooth Stones are smooth! They need to be around for a while before they are ready to launch. They must have had a chance to lose their rough edges by the movement of seasons in life, a connection to tangible efforts, and through the preparation process of God's Supremely Able Helper. An idea to one day help a great cause, for example, may be an Inspired Idea, but it's not smooth enough to do anything with yet. You can't put that in a Slingshot; it won't fly. You can't put a Dream or a Passion in one either. Ideas may lead you to Smooth Stones, and even become them, but they aren't ready to launch when you first find them.

You see what I'm talking about, David? A Dream or a Vision for 'someday' is not able to help you slay a Giant standing right in front of you.

Smooth Stones are Near You!

Which brings us to an important point... *Smooth Stones are often closer than you think.* Even so, they can be hard to spot. You'll need the Supremely Able Helper to open your eyes so you can tell them apart from the rest. Make sure to ask Him for help: to locate a Smooth Stone almost always requires inspiration.

Also, *Smooth Stones are only located near places you should be*, so be careful not to wander off your path. Otherwise, your eyes may play tricks on you. Stones found in other areas may *look* like great ones to use, but they will misfire in *your* Slingshot. That's not a pretty sight with a Giant towering in front of you.

You might not realize this, but surprisingly near you are some Smooth Stones lying around that will make highly effective weapons.

"What! Really? Near me?"

Yes, David.

God Himself has made sure they are there. Many would-be Giant Slayers spend too much time hunting in unusual and distant places: that's unfortunate. Precious time is wasted and the right stones are rarely found there. Another truly remarkable property of Smooth Stones: t*hey not only carry the potential to make things happen for you, they pave the way for others.*

And here's one further truth to keep in mind about Giants and Smooth Stones. Although you will see many Giants in this world, most will not be directly on the road of *your* Special Assignment, but along someone else's.

For example, I have a dear friend who felt inspired to face the Giant Problem of Hunger by starting a non-profit organization. His enterprise feeds the hungry in a unique way. Rather than collecting canned goods or expired baked items, his approach employs scores of volunteers to plant and harvest fresh produce using innovative organic methods. It's a fabulous endeavor which is making a tremendous difference. Since it is such a worthy cause, I could abandon everything else and join that fight full-time. But instead, I've provided special services to support it, I taught my friend the Slingshot Principles, and I remain true to the calling on *my* life. Hunger is his Giant – not mine. I want to help him slay it and I'll stand with him, but I can only do so much.

By all means use the Slingshot Principles to help others deliver impact with their Smooth Stones. However, on the path of *your* Special Assignment, you'll need to choose your own Stone to confront a Giant that stands in your way. At those moments, the Smooth Stones of others won't work. So be on the lookout for your stones, and for the battles where you'll need them.

The right Smooth Stones will help you deliver maximum impact, so let's look for yours. A Smooth Stone is a vehicle that helps you make a difference, an actual tool of decisive action. What does *your*s look like? Look around you, David. See any Smooth Stones? Close your eyes and think about it for a minute. What comes to mind?

Good; that's a start. But there are more…

A Different Way to Find Smooth Stones

Let's explore a different way to find Smooth Stones, which may hold the key for you.

So far we have considered what Stones look like, where to find them, and ways to sift through countless ones to tell them apart. We stressed the importance of asking God to help you choose. We also focused on the 'inspired-ness', the smoothness, and the makeup of the Stones, as well as their potential difference-making impact on both a practical and spiritual level. We even looked at helping others launch theirs.

But right now I want you to look in a completely different direction. Ready? Okay, take a deep breath. Go ahead, take one. *Now, instead of looking for Smooth Stones, I want you to look at Giants…*

Slingshot Secrets
The Paradox of Smooth Stones

"As arrows are in the hand of a mighty man; so are children of the youth." Ps 127:4 KJV

David, be aware that in the same way that children can be like arrows, people can be like Smooth Stones. As an individual is launched effectively into a particular arena or situation, that person's life itself may carry powerful and surprising impact, much like a Smooth Stone.

Smooth Stones are Near Giants

What's standing in your way or in the way of others you care about? Where do you see evidence of Giants at work? What situations don't appear to have the right solution? What seems unjust? Where is there a better way?

Consider the problems of our time, right out in the everyday world. Are they too big? Are they someone else's responsibility? Do you see a leadership void anywhere? Where are the overlooked people? What's keeping you up at night? Are you thinking too small? How about right there, in your community? Do you see certain places where you want to carry God's love, if only you could?

For just a moment, go ahead and forget about how inadequate you may think you are or how the odds would be against you. With your True Identity and Special Assignment as guides, Dream. Look intently around you. Let the problems and opportunities look as big as they are - and then stare right back at them.

Now let's look closer to your heart. You cannot care about everything equally, David; you are drawn to certain things more than others. That's because you were designed that way. What would *you* change if you could? Where would *you* be thrilled to make an impact? Why do *you* want to do that? Sure, there are plenty of issues in the world, but which ones would *you* really like to be involved with, personally? Which issues irritate you more than others? Which are you most passionate about? Where could the world really use an exceptional solution or an exceptional person like you?

Though God has equipped you to make a difference wherever you go, the presence of certain Giants in particular places attracts your attention more than others. It is important to recognize those Giants: they are likely some of the ones that you, personally, are supposed to help get rid of. When you encounter those Giants, you may wonder why other people right next to you aren't doing anything about the situation. Don't they see what's happening – the injustice of it - the opportunity right before them? No, they probably don't. Because that's likely not *their* fight, David - it's *yours*.

Remember, God has placed you here, at this particular time, for a particular reason. Where you live, the people around you, the problems, the possibilities: these form the context of *your* life on earth, David. God could have chosen any place and any time for you, but you are *here*, *now*. It's no accident; He's asking you to step up. Why shrink back or ignore parts of creation facing significant struggles? Bring solutions. Get involved. But not in a way that takes you off course – do it in full Partnership with God and right on the Road of Destiny!

Sometimes you'll locate the most incredible Smooth Stones by simply being the one willing to step up to the Giant. Of course it's important not to rush into every fight. This is one of the hardest lessons to learn: which battles to get involved in and which not to. Once you realize the vast number of possible targets, how can you ever choose between them? It can make you want to ignore them all. It's difficult, right? *But occasionally, it's quite simple.*

Remember how your ancient ancestor David came upon the original Goliath? He was just running an errand his father had given him. Yet God saw to it that along the way, on the path of simply being faithful and obedient, David would cross paths with a Giant he had been prepared to defeat. One minute he had never seen or heard of Goliath, and the next - there he was. The would-be Giant Slayer had not invested months in tracking Goliath, he simply met him on the road of Destiny. But the moment David laid eyes on Goliath and saw no one else stepping up, he knew it was his time.

You see? *That's the power of context.*

So I want you to look around again. A situation right in front of you that is demanding bold action may be no coincidence at all. Maybe you thought you should be doing something more 'spiritual' than solving that practical problem, meeting that need, or building that organization. Be careful: sometimes you can miss your Destiny that way. When you're walking down the right road as best you know how, just being faithful and obedient, God will see to it that you end up in particular places, at key moments.

The secret to seeing the right Smooth Stone can sometimes simply be coming across the right Giant at the right time.

Lastly, keep this in mind. **If your Stone is not wrapped in Prayer, hurled in Partnership with God toward the target, and launched from the path of your Special Assignment, you won't hit the mark.** That goes for business ideas, political campaigns, inspired pursuit of new technologies, outreach efforts, social justice initiatives, new 'ministries', church plants, or special strategies within a larger context of anything you are already doing.

Key to Additional Victories: Finding More Smooth Stones

Have you ever wondered why certain people find ways to win at lots of things, while others don't? Is everything easier for those lucky few? Maybe they received something you and I didn't. Maybe few people would admit to wondering that, but most would love the answer.

I'm not going to try to speak for everyone, but David - I know *you*. You were not created for just one success here and there, but for many. Your potential is far greater than even you have yet understood. To accomplish great things in the everyday world and fulfill your Special Assignment, it will take lots of victories strung together.

And Smooth Stones are surprisingly effective weapons for life's battles: learning to choose the right ones will help you become a great champion; different ones give you the potential to win different battles. Finding even *one* in a pinch is remarkable, but knowing where to find others any time you need them - *that* is truly life-changing. The important thing is not simply to be able to pick one out with a lucky guess, but to master choosing the right one for the right situation.

One thing is certain, David: we need many more Smooth Stones hurtling through the air toward their intended targets, all over the world. The world needs you to find and launch yours - and to help others do the same.

Smooth Stones Checklist

Here is a potent checklist that will help you recognize Smooth Stones. Any that you choose should meet *all* of these criteria.

☐ **Find it in the right place** - Located along the path of Destiny, in a sphere where you can use at least *some* Skills you have developed over time. It should help you fulfill part of your Special Assignment.

☐ **Make sure it's got substance** - A specific means, a way to solve a problem, create value, or advance an effort you are passionate about. It might be a company, a cause, a campaign, a certain initiative or way to do something, but it's specific and has substance. It is work that you can partner with God in and give him glory when it succeeds. *Though many Smooth Stones were once ideas, until they take on shape and form they are not Smooth Stones.* Remember, the Slingshot Principles are for Smooth Stones, not ideas. (Example: This book in present form is a Smooth Stone; the idea I had to write it years ago was not. An actual villa where Kingdom leaders can rest on sabbatical is a Smooth Stone; the dream to someday build one is not.)

☐ **Make sure it fits you** - Allows you to express your True Identity and is consistent with it. Doesn't require hyper-conformity or compromise.

- ☐ **Confirm it with the Lord** - Something you are convinced that God approves of, that you sense His leading about on some level.

- ☐ **Make sure it can be aimed properly** - When it hits the mark, it makes a difference for the Kingdom of God and benefits others, not just yourself. Be able to answer this question: *Of what benefit will it be to the Kingdom of God when this Smooth Stone hits the mark?*

- ☐ **Make sure it's smooth enough** - Not too rough or half-baked. It's been around long enough to become smoothed; it's been honed, one way or another.

We need many more Smooth Stones hurtling through the air toward their intended targets, all over the world. The world needs you to find and launch yours - and to help others do the same.

There are only so many Smooth Stones you yourself can launch, so you will want each one to count. That doesn't mean you can't grab handfuls for practice. But remember, in real battles, valuable things are usually at stake, so choose wisely.

Chapter 10
Key Takeaways & Giant Slayer Tips

- A Smooth Stone is an **inspired means** to deliver an **exceptional impact**.

- Without the right Smooth Stone you won't **hit the mark**, no matter how good you become with a Slingshot.

- They come in **many shapes and sizes**, but their intended use is the same: (1) to help you deliver an exceptional impact which is part of your Special Assignment, (2) to displace opposing forces, and (3) to glorify God.

- Smooth Stones have **physical substance**. Inspired Ideas, Dreams, and Visions by themselves, therefore, are not Smooth Stones. (Remember, the 4 main Keys to the Slingshot apply to Smooth Stones, not to ideas alone.)

- Smooth Stones are often **surprisingly nearby**.

- Smooth Stones not only carry the potential to make things happen for you, they **pave the way for others**.

- **Use the checklist** to help you recognize the right ones.

- Smooth Stones require a **Slingshot**, and a Slingshot requires Smooth Stones.

Chapter 11
Knowing When to Step Up

"There's an opportune time to do things, a right time for everything on the earth..." *Eccl. 3:1 MSG*

Picture this somewhat typical American family scene. At 7:40 AM a woman swoops her baby up with one arm, grabs a check to be mailed, and hurries down the stairs exclaiming over her shoulder, "Make sure you're ready to go when I get back at 9:30." Strapping the child securely into a well-worn car seat, with what looks like spaghetti stuck to one of the arms, she flicks it out of the way and yells to her two other daughters that they should already be in the car. All still fumbling with hair accessories, everyone jumps in and the foursome speeds away. Coffee spills slightly at some point in the action, but blends in with where it leaked out the other day.

One child to day camp, one to a friend's house across town, then to the store with baby to pick up a few things for company coming over that night. As she checks out, the phone jingles: it's her mother-in-law hoping for a commitment to a family gathering next Easter. While the two discuss this possibility, the other line rings: a friend needs to borrow an extra large pot for the big party her family is having tomorrow, because her husband is making chili to serve 25. But it needs to simmer overnight, so she has to have it right away. Thinking quickly, the woman gracefully makes arrangements for both situations as she continues to the post office. From there she hits another store for diapers and then a second one to grab printer ink, run dry from too many unauthorized coloring sheets.

Looking down at her watch, her face flushes just a bit as she realizes she'll now have to race home to take her son to the birthday party, and probably be slightly late. (Why was the checkout lady shooting the breeze with the couple in front of her for what seemed like 7 minutes? That's annoying...) Now she won't be able to make it to the beginning of exercise class. Right then, out of nowhere, a thought pops into her head and she wonders if the words *summer* and *vacation* really go together and who first thought of that term.

Racing home, she leaves the car running with baby in tow, rushes inside for a quick pitstop, and shouts up through her son's closed door, "You better be ready to go!" After coming out of the bathroom and not hearing any signs of movement, she vaults two stairs at a time to his room, busting in to find him without shirt or shoes, playing video games. Drinking from the deep reserves that only a mom can, she finds the moxie to not explode and instead sternly declares, "We've got to go NOW. Your sister is in the car and we're running late".

He mentions something about not being able to find his favorite shirt and then a funny look comes on his face. With no warning, the ten-year-old boy looks up and says, "Mom, we need to talk."

"That's great, son, but it will have to wait until we get in the car. Shirt and shoes. Let's go. We've got to be at the party by 9:45," she adds, as the tension in her voice rises.

"No, I need to talk to you *now*," he insists.

Dreading the thought of being late, and hating another delay, but knowing that this might actually be at least somewhat important, she sighs, "Okay, okay son, what is it?"

"Mom, I've been thinking. Can we go get that new baseball bat I told you I wanted *right now?* I can use it next season too."

As if momentarily shaking off a surprise blow to the head, his mother quickly recovers and fires back, "We're late; you're not ready; that store is 20 minutes away; the bat you want is $300; and you ask me <u>now</u>?!!! Son, any chances you had of getting that bat just went *way down!*"

"Uh, what does this have to do with slaying Giants?"

When slaying a Giant, David, timing is crucial. The boy failed to assess his situation and pick the right time to ask his mother for the bat; in fact, he was clueless. That time seemed to him as good as any other, but his very poor timing may well have cost him the outcome he hoped for. The sad truth is, *if he'd pursued his desire at a different moment, things might have worked out in his favor.*

The Power of Timing

Some would-be Giant Slayers have a hard time figuring out when to step up, and when not to. What keeps them from experiencing major breakthroughs is simply poor Timing. Whether you are learning to golf, disciplining a child, building a ministry, trying to land a promotion, approaching a friend with an idea, advancing a new initiative, seeking investors, serving a meal at the local homeless shelter, putting an Anniversary Card on the table, or slaying Giants - Timing matters greatly.

In the story of Queen Esther, it wasn't Courage alone that saved the day: it was acting at the right moment, within a certain window of opportunity. You and I need to recognize these kinds of windows in our own lives. Here is what Mordecai said to Esther about timing:

> "The fact is, even if you remain silent now, someone else will help and rescue the Jews, but you and your relatives will die. And who knows, you may have gained your royal position for a time like this."
> *Est. 4:14 GOD'S WORD*

In other words: "Act now. If you don't, you'll probably miss a divine opportunity which God has specially positioned you for - and you'll also suffer serious consequences."

The bigger the stakes, the more important it is to make sure you understand the right time to act. Rescheduling a hair appointment because of bad timing is one thing, but stepping up to a Giant at the wrong time can cost you dearly - even when you've chosen the right Giant. *To slay Giants, you'll need to not only take decisive action with your Smooth Stone and Slingshot, but take it at the right moment.* How will you know when it's the right time to step out? Are you sure that's your Giant? While everyone says *time* is precious, *Timing* is too.

> *Timing takes practice, awareness, and sensitivity to the leading of the Supremely Able Helper, all of which can be developed.*

Since we entertained the subject of baseball, David, let's look at one more example of the importance of Timing. Have you ever noticed what's called the final box score? It's a grid with numbers that tells you at a glance what happened during a particular baseball game. By looking at the numbers, you can tell how many hits each team got, as well as the final score. In some cases, this final box score is puzzling. One team can have 9 hits and the other 13, yet the one with less hits won 8-2.

How can that happen?

In baseball, you would think that a team hitting the ball more would win. It makes sense: after all, a big part of baseball is hitting the ball! *But when a team with fewer hits actually wins by a big margin* (or any margin for that matter), most often there are two factors at work: one is the *type* of hit and the other is *Timing*. Obviously if a team has only 9 hits, but eight of them are homeruns, and the other team has 12 hits that are all singles, that's one way a team with less hits could beat a team with more.

The other way is less obvious and more intriguing: *Timing*. In the event neither team has a type-of-hit advantage, how then could the team with fewer hits win? The answer is usually found in Timing: WHEN the team gets their hits. *Hitting at the most opportune times can mean the difference between winning and losing.* If the bases are loaded when someone hits a double, runs will score. However, if nobody is on base, no runs are scored.

The only difference? Timing.

So by stringing together a few well-*timed* hits, a team with fewer hits can beat a team with more. In fact, hitting at key moments is why certain players are considered 'sluggers' or 'clutch performers', and others aren't. Hitting anytime is great, but hitting *when it really counts* produces greater effect. Certain players not only know what to do and how to do it, but have a knack for WHEN to do it. So it is in many areas of life. A person who understands not only *what* to do and *how* to do it, but WHEN to do it, frequently enjoys a strategic advantage.

Set Times

David, you're going to need this type of edge to slay Goliaths and accomplish great things in the everyday world. But beware, timing is tricky, and often misunderstood.

Sure, occasionally you just show up in the right place at the right time without knowing exactly how you got there. It's as if a number of factors beyond your control simply lined up for you. (They probably did.) When that happens, it's a great feeling; a series of events may unfold even better than you dreamt they might. This is exactly what happened to your ancestor, the eventual King David. God had made sure that young David had the prior training experiences (the bear and the lion, the time alone with God) necessary to prepare him to defeat Goliath, and David – totally clueless about the battle with an evil Giant coming up - had very wisely taken advantage of all the 'slack time' in his 'dead-end job' as a shepherd boy, and Focused on becoming expertly Skilled with his Slingshot and Smooth Stones.

God makes certain that each of us has some of these experiences. *There are set times of divine opportunity which He controls completely. We don't know exactly how He brings them about, but He does.*

How you respond during those moments, David, is of course up to you, but you need to recognize them and rise to the occasion. That's when you summon Courage, grab some Smooth Stones and a Slingshot, and step up. God has a complete corner on the market for this kind of Timing.

Variable Times

However, there are many kinds of important battles where Timing isn't so clear. It's those that I want to look at for just a minute. As we do, keep this in mind: what further complicates Timing is when there are *multiple actions to take that must be done in a certain order* - the *sequence* - to create maximum effect. It sounds funny, but what if the Israelites at Jericho had shouted first, then blown the trumpets, and later marched around Jericho seven times. That wouldn't have had the same impact, would it?

There are times in life when you need to be especially tuned in, David, as to whether the time is right to act. Do you remember when Jesus was invited to go to a big celebration that others thought he should attend? We know he wasn't against celebrating, yet he surprised everyone by refusing to go. Why? Here's what he said:

> "Jesus replied, "Now is not the right time for me to go, but you can go anytime. The world can't hate you, but it does hate me because I accuse it of doing evil. You go on. I'm not going to this festival, because my time has not yet come." *John 7:6-8 NLT*

What I want you to see here is how Jesus was aware of the Timing in His life set by God, according to His Special Assignment. **Having knowledge about God's Timing affected his actions and choices in the everyday world.** You see, David, some Giant Slayers get into trouble by not bothering to learn more about Timing. They can't tell different times apart, and so they just pick one. What a shame to turn victory into defeat by neglecting such a small but crucial factor!

Timing takes practice, awareness, and sensitivity to the leading of the Supremely Able Helper, all of which can be developed.

So Far, So Good

We've looked at Timing that is completely beyond your control because you aren't even aware of it: a set time, a huge moment that you just suddenly find yourself in, which God arranged without your knowledge. In that kind of Timing there isn't much you can do, except to have followed God as best you could before arriving there. Then you should be ready for whatever you see.

Next we looked at the set Timing of God that it <u>is possible to be aware of</u>, so you can avoid taking action at odds with His plan; trust me, David, you do NOT want to do that! *You and I must learn to recognize and cooperate with <u>His</u> times and seasons*: when to act and when not to; when the time is right and when it isn't. That kind of awareness only comes from an intimate relationship with God.

But what about those times when you don't sense any clear direction from God, yet must act? At one extreme, hyper-spiritual people might suggest that you should have perfectly clear direction from God at all times in everything. So before you can put on blue socks or green ones, perhaps you should call in sick until an angel reveals which is the pair of the day! Though that is a cynical example, the reality is that *God does not send complete instructions for every single decision* that we must make. At the opposite extreme, other Kingdom citizens continually barrel right past virtually *all* decisions without *ever* stopping to inquire of the Lord. Neither approach will help you slay Giants, and both of them will invite catastrophe into your life.

Vacation Lessons

While this next example is more about listening for God's direction than Timing per se, it will help you see something important about Timing. One year I felt like it was time to take my family on vacation. I had two ideas about where to go, and wasn't certain which place would be more fun. I researched a few interesting highlights about each destination, and was still torn. So believe it or not, I asked the Lord where to go.

Guess what I heard from Him? Nothing!

But - fancying myself as a 'spiritual' guy - I was certain I was 'supposed' to go one place and not the other. So I kept praying. Finally one day I had an impression which went something like this: "Where would *you* like to go? Go there." So I picked one, and we all had a great time.

But that isn't the end of the story. **Pay very close attention here, David.**

Our next family vacation appeared to be another completely optional choice, just like the last one. I could have assumed, "I guess God never cares where I go on vacation, so I will *assume* that this time I can also choose wherever I want to go." Fortunately though, I still listened for God's direction as I mulled over options. The funny thing is, this time I felt extremely certain that I was <u>not</u> to go to one place, and that I should go to the other. So I acted accordingly.

Might something bad have happened if I hadn't inquired of the Lord and we had gone to the other place? I don't know - but I do know this: not only did we have an amazing time going where I felt led, but our time also included several divine appointments we otherwise would not have had.

The lesson is not: "Pray about where to go on vacation," it's: *If you don't check for messages, you might not realize there is one in your inbox.* Don't assume: ask. That goes for Timing as well.

Choosing the Best Time to Act

But what happens in situations when you do ask, and you hear just plain nothing, yet you simply have to act, because the time for decision has arrived? What then? This is not farfetched. It happens daily. Sometimes you simply have to use your best judgment, (1) <u>drawing upon what you have learned</u>, and (2) <u>paying close attention to certain indicators</u> as you move along. Life doesn't always allow you time to come to a complete stop for every decision. The more responsibility you have, the more decisions you must make – every day. You won't have complete instructions for all of them.

For example, let's say your company is releasing a new product and there are three different plans on the table. As director, you must decide which plan to adopt. You've been pondering the options for a few weeks, prayed about them, yet you don't have a solution. Today is the day you committed to having made a decision, so your company could have enough time to respond.

- Plan A (30 days) is the most aggressive timeline, and declares that immediate action is required to capitalize on anticipated demand for the new product, and to generate near-term revenue.

- Plan B (60 days) supposes that there is not enough awareness in the market yet, and that additional pre-marketing is necessary before launch.

- Plan C (120 days) suggests that demand for the product will multiply more rapidly if it is released with a companion product, not due out until Spring.

Which is the best time to act? Of course there are many possible reason which could affect the choice, but the specifics are not as important to this example as how to approach it.

What have you learned in the past from similar situations? Does experience provide any clues? Did you learn something from the Lord previously about this? Then make the most informed decision you can with the information available, *paying close attention to any guidance you may receive from the Supremely Able Helper as you move forward.* (Hopefully you have already asked trusted associates to also be praying for guidance and clarity for you.)

BUT – as you take those first few steps, LISTEN and be very aware of how you feel in your heart. If you lose the sense of peace you normally have – STOP. You are probably either going the wrong way or moving at the wrong time. But if peace remains, keep moving forward.

In conclusion, be aware that Timing is often a crucial determining factor in victory or defeat, and be aware of the need to frequently ask God about what is the best *time* to act concerning things you undertake. That's the best advice I can give you, whether you're slaying Giants or creating strategic plans.

But don't worry: remember, you are not in this battle alone, and you haven't simply been tossed into the arena and left to your own wisdom and devices. The King has promised that if you trust in Him with all your heart, He will make your paths straight, and that the Supremely Able Helper will guide you into all truth.

Chapter 11

Key Takeaways & Giant Slayer Tips

☑ Even when everything else is aligned perfectly, pursuing something at **the wrong time can cause failure,** when success would have otherwise been the result.

☑ The bigger the stakes, the more important it is to make sure you understand **the right time to act**.

☑ There are some **set times** that God alone controls.

☑ Other aspects of Timing take practice, awareness, and sensitivity. Ask God whether the time is right, and then <u>listen</u> for His answer. Learn to **become more aware of Timing** in what you do.

☑ Timing also comes into play with multiple events; some situations **require a phased approach**.

☑ **Timing & *Sequence* often work together**; not only 'when', but 'in what order'.

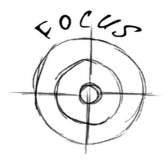

Chapter 12
An Unsung Hero

"So let's keep focused on that goal, those of us who want everything God has for us. If any of you have something else in mind, something less than total commitment, God will clear your blurred vision — you'll see it yet! Now that we're on the right track, let's stay on it."
Phil. 3:15-16 MSG

"**W**ait a minute. Slingshot Principles? Smooth Stones? Giants? I think I'm getting somewhere, but it still seems hazy."

I'm glad you pointed that out, David, and it's okay that some things still seem unclear. We're going to shed more light on your path by introducing an unsung hero into your story; he is an amazing character. To help you move forward, meet true Focus: *concentrated, sustained attention and effort* on the *right things.*

Now, these days everyone is talking about Vision, and you likely already have one yourself. (And the real question is not so much whether you have one, but are you fulfilling it?) Hopefully, working through this book is helping to make your Vision clearer. Yet if not, don't worry:

when you arrive at the intersection of your True Identity and Special Assignment (if you haven't yet) - as the Great Entrance to Destiny appears – you'll *catch some glimpses of your long-range future.* Those glimpses will cause your heart to thrill, and you'll sense new strength arising in you. Maybe you've already been there; but that was just a taste. Being at that epic intersection, even for a moment, and then entering into your Partnership with God, results in Vision forming: the right kind of Vision. Then, once you identify a particular Smooth Stone and a Target, things become even clearer.

Why Vision Alone Often Falters

But Vision, <u>without the unsung hero Focus</u>, goes nowhere. Vision is like a boat that looks impressive and has great potential, but without Focus, sailing round and round in the harbor is all it ever does - if it even leaves the dock.

Focus can help you sail out on the open water into your greater future. *Just staring at your destination doesn't bring you toward it;* that only makes things blur eventually. Instead, with Focus, you act smartly and intentionally in the here and now - consistently. Keeping your bigger Vision fixed in your heart and mind is certainly needed - just don't let that be the full extent of what you do.

Think about what you're doing now, David. In fact, what *are* you doing? As you have believed God to carry you further than you can get on your own, *are you also doing what it takes on your end* to move forward? Find a way to mix Focus with the Slingshot Principles and others hidden in this how-to-story, and you'll experience major progress. Try it, and you'll see.

Bringing Focus to Life

Let's look at a story that I think will help you to harness Focus: a story about this book. Please keep in mind that when these words were written, no book had been printed, no publishers were considering it, and the author (me) was a *complete* unknown.

> ### Slingshot Secrets
> ## The 'Other' Slingshot Effect
>
> ...the Holy Spirit spoke: "Take Barnabas and Saul and commission them for the work I have called them to do." Acts 13:2 MSG
>
> David, when you personally harness Focus, that's powerful. But when others also discern your True Identity & Special Assignment and come alongside to commission you toward that Focus, this creates another type of Slingshot Effect.

Put yourself in my shoes a few years ago, and dream my Inspired Dream for a minute:

The Inspired Dream of Smooth Stones and This Book

Let's suppose that in my Inspired Dream, my 'Vision', this book is the beginning phase of helping Kingdom citizens to step out in ways they never have before: to partner with God, defeat Goliaths, and accomplish great things in the everyday world. I mean REALLY do it: not just talk about it, read other people's accounts, or wonder if it's actually possible.

As crazy as that might sound to you - and trust me, sometimes it seemed crazy to me! - let's also suppose that I was told that this book is itself a demonstration of how to launch a Smooth Stone in Partnership with God.

Let's further suppose that part of the dream was that God's Supremely Able Helper will not only work through the book, but also *with* readers in miraculous ways, beyond the words on the page, doing what only He can do in people's lives. Let's imagine that these people are a generation of God-fearing believers with a combined Giant-slaying-potential so massive that, when they awaken to it and see how to lay hold of it, they will literally change the entire world.

"Oh, come on Rick," you might say, *"surely that's ridiculous!"*

Maybe so, but just suppose…

So, how on earth could *this* Smooth Stone hit its mark?

Now you may or may not think such a grand result is farfetched: after all, like winning the lottery, some unknown authors do achieve great success. But let me explain just how farfetched it really was. Practically speaking, the odds are *virtually nil* of a totally unknown author, without special connections or unique status - just your average guy - publishing a first book that causes anything more than a silent ripple. Even in an entire lifetime, to write *any* book with acceptable sales figures is a rare feat, even with significant support from the 'right' people. In terms of hardcopies, .03 percent of all submissions (only 3 books out of 10,000 !!!) are accepted for publication. Of those, 9 out of every 10 published novels fail to pay back production costs.[4] And in the non-fiction arena, some industry experts[5] consider 'success' to be sales of a measly 7500 copies. Think about how few copies sold that is: there are some individual Base Camps with more than 7500 readers in them!

With this book I also faced unexpected health issues, hosts of naysayers, and self-doubt – but I kept moving forward anyway. And there were other obstacles: this book presents (1) a *new paradigm* on (2) a somewhat *controversial topic* in (3) an *unconventional manner*. Without an unusually favorable reception, any *one* of those three elements could have limited the project to obscurity.

And - if this book actually does contain keys that will help many Kingdom citizens defeat Goliaths and accomplish great things that glorify God - Giants might prefer that it never even got published at all, eh? After all, it's better to stop something cold than take a risk. So it's probably safe to assume that there were also *spiritual* reasons that this

4 Source: www.tarakharper.com
5 Source: Authors Guild, www.authorsguild.org

book hitting its target was the greatest of long shots. And yet somehow the book is here, in your hands.

Perhaps that's somewhat like your story, David - or your story-to-be. Perfect! Your Partner specializes in impossible victories!

A Pattern of Focus

In writing this book, Focus helped produce smaller victories along the way, and those small victories eventually led to a bigger breakthrough. And Focus will do the same for you.

(By the way, *my progress means almost nothing to me without yours; your progress is what this book is all about, David*.)

Here's how Focus played into my story; catch the pattern I used to move forward.

I have worked the better part of my life to improve my writing and teaching skills. In the process I have written articles, blogs, magazine ads, web content, specialized workshops, radio spots, product descriptions, business plans, strategic plans, marketing plans, video scripts, corporate training materials, personal stories, and much more. I have taught workshops, clients, sermons, e-learning modules, corporate training, small groups, seminars, and my own children.

For every word that has appeared in public, countless more haven't. For every person who told me they loved my teaching and got so much out of it, two others looked puzzled, and had questions I thought I had answered in the session they were just in. Mastery of both disciplines still eludes me, but I continue to improve by practicing, *focusing my efforts on these disciplines*.

I continued to Focus while dozens of people put forward numerous ideas that could have sidetracked or discouraged me. As well, I did not just cavalierly leave everything up to God - as if *that's* Faith - and act like nothing I did was important, expecting my destination to mysteriously appear one day. No, my Faith supplied energy for me to act.

Because I chose to invest time in skill development and pursuit of this Vision, there were other things I had to pass up. For example, I spent who-knows-how-many hours studying a wonderful book called *Keys to Great Writing,* by Stephen Wilbers. While I labored over sentence variety and the rhythm of my writing on evenings and weekends, most people were having fun, watching TV, sharing family times, or telling me I was working too hard. Yet, in my heart, I believed I was focusing on the right thing during that season of my life. When I did sometimes get off track and found myself losing my Focus, I didn't allow myself to remain off-course.

Significant progress requires sacrifice and determination, David. This is particularly true when you want to step into a major breakthrough in life, as major breakthroughs often require periods of exceptionally sustained Focus. Yet by definition, *Focus can only be applied effectively to a few things at once.* You have to discover which things to keep in view, and then stick with them longer than you probably want to: that's Focus.

Sometimes when you <u>simplify</u> what you are trying to accomplish – and then <u>Focus</u> - only then will breakthrough come.

Setting Priorities

I want to assure you, David, there were many times I didn't *feel* like writing or teaching. The process of creating this book was a combination of a few mountaintop experiences together with many basic, workman-like days. This was part of *my* preparation to defeat a certain Giant, a Goliath who has tricked countless believers into settling for far less than what is possible in life! I am fed up with seeing great people with Inspired Dreams held back by that windbag. In partnership with God, you CAN dare to step up and expect exceptional results.

One thing that will help you stay focused, David, is to remember your future reward, while you faithfully tend sheep and practice your harp. For example, my reward is facilitating personal breakthrough for believers, generating Kingdom Advancement in the here and now, and whatever will come my way in eternity for having completed this Special Assignment. (Though I'm not completely sure what the reward is, I'm definitely looking forward to it!) I keep these rewards in front of me in all I do; I Focus on them! And it's not wrong to do that; in fact the

Inspired Guidebook encourages us to do so.

Now let me give you an even deeper view of the priorities you should Focus on.

For Kingdom citizens, *Focus is doing your best to pay attention to and act upon whatever the King highlights as most important - at any given time and place.* That's the truest form of Focus: *setting your priorities by His,* seeking first His Kingdom, and asking Him what He wants you to do to help make His Kingdom more tangible here on Earth.

A Personal Mission Statement

It can be amazingly productive to spend a few minutes crafting a personal mission statement (which does not need to be set in stone for eternity); this can help you stay focused on what is most important in a given season, or even over years. There are many variations on how to write one, and I highly recommend finding a format you like, and then using it.

For a number of years, the statement I used to guide me was: "*developing business & business people for Kingdom advancement.*" Recently, it has become: "*to release destiny to an emerging generation of Kingdom citizens.*" That's the simple, over arching version. And I also have a more detailed version which adds a lot more to the 'how' I am going about it:[6]

> "*To release destiny to an emerging generation of Kingdom citizens; to help them partner with God, win strategic victories and accomplish great things – through writing, teaching, coaching, consulting, unmistakable demonstration which points to God, business growth & creativity; to raise up a 'Tribe of Giant Slayers' with worldwide impact.*"

If you think some of that sounds familiar; GREAT! Writing this book is supposed to be closely in line with my mission!

While it's not the goal of this book to help you merely *discover* Destiny, but to help you connect the dots toward *reaching* yours – here are a few thoughts about writing personal mission statements, just to point you in

---

6 If you would like more detail on writing a Personal Mission Statement, the companion workbook that is available separately at www.tribeofgiantslayers.com provides it, including many more examples.

the right direction.

Ideally you want your personal mission statement to act as a compass for your life. It's easy to over-think the process of creating a solid statement, yet at the same time, you want it to be accurate. So ask the Supremely Able Helper for assistance as you work. What do you feel called to do, and for whom? Totally general statements that could apply to any Kingdom citizen usually don't provide as much thrust, such as "*to be a servant leader wherever I can.*" Shorter is usually better, and make your statement as memorable as possible; in finished form the statement should inspire *you*. <u>And, once you complete your mission statement, it's a great idea to keep it somewhere you can see it regularly, ideally every day.</u>

To use another personal example to help you choose Kingdom priorities: it's not that being a successful author/motivator and providing well for my family to enjoy life aren't important to me, it's just that those things are not my primary Focus. They are a *by-product* of what I'm actually focused on: releasing Destiny to an emerging generation of believers. If I complete the main assignment, the other things also fall into place. What I mean, David, is that *you must choose your focus and priorities with extreme care, or they will lead you astray.*

Once you gain God's insight and set your direction, stay focused. Of course you may need to make course corrections along the way, but don't use that as an excuse for chasing rabbits instead of sticking to what's most important.

Don't let anyone talk you out of what you know that God has put in your heart to do.

'Wisdom' in Western Virginia

To stay focused on the right things, you'll need wisdom from others. By the same token, *you'll need to filter bad advice.* This requires both courage and discernment. On occasion, great wisdom will come from sources which you'll be tempted to ignore. (If it is truly insight from the Lord and intended for you, then you'd better listen - even if it's coming from a person you don't get along with, or an employee, or a child!)

On the other hand, sometimes 'together' people, whom you respect, will unintentionally give bad advice. When that happens, you can lose momentum – <u>as I know all too well; following bad advice, however well-intentioned, can cost you a lot - and cause you to lose your Focus.</u>

You see, not long ago my family and enjoyed a wonderful, extended stay in the mountains of western Virginia. That part of the country is filled with incredible views, charm, wildlife, and plentiful advice. One day the subject of the local deer population came up; this naturally led to a discussion of why there are so many 'deer incidents' on the roads there, and what to do to avoid hitting one. A confident woman piped up brightly, "When you see a deer on the side of the road, all you need to do is keep moving at the same speed, and the deer will adjust. But if you try to slam on the brakes or do anything sudden, that's when it gets spooked." That sounded sensible to me. (Unfortunately!)

Early one morning a few days later, before dawn, we headed out on the road to family adventure. My wife and I commented on how smoothly the departure had gone with our three children. (Those of you who have kids know how tricky smooth early-morning departures can be!) As we sipped the perfect coffee we had prepared for the road, we both felt smug, almost giddy, about getting out the door so easily; it was going to be a great day! Coming around the bend, in the headlights I suddenly spotted a deer stirring on the side of the road. Instinctively I moved to slam on the brakes. But then I recalled the 'sensible' advice I had been given: "Keep moving at the same speed." So I resisted the urge to brake, and just "kept on truckin".

BAM!!!!!!!! The large buck lurched right into the front of our van, completely ignoring the woman's advice. The nerve of that creature! If I had only listened to my instincts and quickly slowed down, I would have had plenty of time to avoid the accident. But I didn't, so I paid the price. Though fortunately we were all okay, our vehicle was out of commission and the trip was over until we could make other arrangements. Four thousand dollars in repair costs and a huge hassle later, I had once again learned the lesson about following bad advice.

It's easy to become either too unteachable or too open-minded: neither works. Finding and keeping balance between the two requires

Focus. *Unwise* counsel will pull you away from your True Identity & Special Assignment, *but <u>without Wise Counsel</u> you won't arrive at your destination either.* You must learn to tell them apart. (Hint: Ask the Supremely Able Helper; he's a lot smarter than we are!)

A Catalyst & Accelerator

Though we've already discussed the importance of Skill in a previous chapter, I want to point out that Focus helps *accelerate* the development of Skill. Unfortunately, too many Kingdom citizens discount the extended process of skill development: our worlds tend instead to be full of half-baked projects. If we started less, we'd finish more.

A valuable truth about Focus is that, when you combine it with other success factors, it acts as a powerful catalyst, a force multiplier. Join your Focus with Prayer, Courage, Skill, and Unconventional Tactics, for example, and your Smooth Stone is likely to hit its intended target sooner than you think.

The Rising Tennis Star

As an example of the value of both simplifying your Focus and combining it with some other Slingshot Principles, let's look at the modern day women's tennis star, Serena Williams. In addition to winning hard-fought championships around the world for many years and (when this book was written) being the highest earning female athlete of all-time, Serena later became an author, a clothing designer, a spokesperson, part-owner of the Miami Dolphins, an actress, an entertainer, and even a social activist – and that's just a partial list!

But during her early years, Serena was intently focused on becoming the most successful tennis player she could be. Many people don't know that she's actually more passionate about some of her other interests, but initially she stayed committed to developing her talents in that single arena, which led to mastery of it - and thus a much higher impact. Without breaking through in tennis, many of Serena's other opportunities never would have come about. **If instead of simplifying, she had tried** to accomplish *all* her goals at the same time early in life, she likely would have achieved none.

My point, David, is <u>not</u> that you need to become famous as a springboard to other achievements - because God's Special Assignment for you has its own unique path, which may or may not include celebrity. The point is that developing your God-given Skills to a high-impact level takes Focus, which can then lead to great things. While right now - for a variety of reasons - you might not be able to pursue just one area exclusively, perhaps you can simplify things a bit.

Let's face it: it's tough to keep *one* longer-term objective in view, let alone many. Most people try to accomplish too many things at the same time - <u>especially</u> early in life. That usually leads to only average results across the board, and thus frustration. While it's true that we all need to explore options and grow as a person, at some point you must set priorities and Focus on them: that's just life. Stories of people who appear to accomplish everything overnight, or who came to great influence with supposedly little effort and focus, mislead people. Reading too many of those accounts can leave you drifting in the realm of indecision. There you start living as if you expect God to help you win the lottery, rather than being faithful to invest the talents He's given you into opportunities at hand. Remember, David:

Sometimes one major breakthrough leads to others, but the first one usually takes longer and requires more FOCUS than you think. Determine the right priorities, then Focus and seek to excel in them as you walk with God.

Along the way, God will present you with opportunities to step up and win smaller battles, and then ultimately defeat a Giant, so be ready. Whether your Smooth Stone is a non-profit initiative, a business idea, prayer movement, role to step into, or other strategy from heaven - whatever it is - Focus will help you hit your target. Take it with you wherever you go.

If you will take these lessons about Focus to heart, David, then your greater future will soon be knocking at the door.

Chapter 12

Key Takeaways & Giant Slayer Tips

- Focus is *concentrated, **sustained attention and effort** on the right things.*

- Vision **without Focus** usually goes nowhere.

- **Major breakthroughs often are preceded** by periods of exceptionally sustained Focus.

- Focus acts as **a catalyst** or acceleration factor.

- A solid **Personal Mission Statement** can be a powerful tool to help keep you on track!

- Sometimes it's necessary to **simplify before you can multiply**.

- The truest form of Focus is **setting your priorities around God's.**

Chapter 13
Bellowing at the Beast

"You will also decree a thing, and it will be established for you; and light will shine on your ways." *Job 22:28 NASV*

Enough! It's time, David. Take your Smooth Stone and Slingshot and run toward the fight. Do what you came here to do: WIN the fight of your life!

You've got all you need – ignore all those folks who don't think you stand a chance; their hearts are too small to see what God will do through you. Once you defeat this Giant, David, your life will never be the same! In case you start having second thoughts, remember how significant a breakthrough this victory will be! That can keep you pushing forward when fear wants to push you back. There's just one last thing…

Though it may seem unwise, or arrogant, or perhaps even reckless, **it's time to bellow at the beast.**

"Uhhh -WHAT? You mean shout at the Giant? No thanks! You must be crazy."

I'm not, nor am I kidding.

"*Well I can't see how yelling at him will help - and it might stir him up. And why on earth would I want to do <u>that</u>? Besides, isn't the element of surprise on my side? You know, 'cause maybe he was expecting someone bigger or differently equipped.*"

David, you've come this far, so I urge you not to get distracted right when victory is nearly in your grasp. As incredible as it seems, what comes out

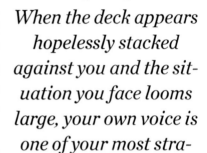

When the deck appears hopelessly stacked against you and the situation you face looms large, your own voice is one of your most strategic secret weapons.

of your mouth *can* affect the outcome of this fight. Yes, when the deck appears hopelessly stacked against you and the situation you face looms large, your own voice is one of your most strategic secret weapons. But it's not a matter of talking your way *out of or into something*. Hardly – it's a matter of talking your way *through*: discovering how to deliver words that *penetrate* the situation.

"*Exactly how does one harness this power? How can we transfer mere words into a potent weapon that turns the tables even on Giants? Is that even possible?*"

Yes, David, it is.

But first, we need to correct a big problem. *There's a lot of bad advice out there about how this works*, so the waters have been muddied. If this practice were clearly understood and done properly, a lot more Davids like you would be fulfilling Destiny, and a lot more Giants would be surrendering ground. To make matters worse, it's not that the wrong advice produces nothing, it actually produces something you and I would rather it didn't: **it produces parrots, not Giant Slayers**. A parrot can repeat what it has heard, which may sound quite impressive, but when pressed, the parrot will either fly away or just keep repeating the same things over and over. The parrot's words never make much of a difference in its life, and the parrot rarely experiences lasting change.

Now don't get me wrong: a parrot is a cool bird and all, colorful and smart, if maybe just a little annoying at times – but it is definitely *not* the creature you want to emulate when challenging a Giant. If you want to slay Giants and go on to accomplish other great things in partnership with God, you'll have to learn to roar like a lion.

Harnessing the Power of Decree

It's time to revisit a lost art: harnessing the power of an Inspired Decree. Once again, this is a place where we Kingdom citizens can tap into a spectacular advantage – but we often don't.

Have you noticed that when some people speak, situations change and mountains move, yet when others *say practically the same things,* their words sound hollow and fall to the ground just after escaping their lips? What do those in the first group know, that the rest don't? For example, in the movie *Braveheart*, do you think that the words of William Wallace (played by Mel Gibson), words that stirred an outmatched, underequipped army to fight bravely for Scottish independence, could have been delivered with similar effect by *anyone* able simply to parrot those words? No way.

Now keep in mind that I'm not mocking the parrot: being able to accurately declare passages directly from the Inspired Guidebook is certainly important. **What I *am* saying is that there is *more to decrees* than mere duplication and repetition**. It's one thing to recite something; quite another to decree it. So let's find out what needs to accompany our words for them to literally penetrate the atmosphere of our lives, and influence outcomes.

First of all, what is a decree? A decree is a royal edict. It's an authoritative proclamation or command. It is not a random statement, but one sent forth with a purpose. The decree itself carries weight to accomplish something; it's dripping with power. Yet if it's not uttered by someone with the proper authority, nothing happens.

Remember in Luke chapter 2, when a "decree went out from Caesar Augustus that all the world should be taxed…and then all went to be taxed," there was a direct connection between what was stated and what happened next. That's the power of a decree. It literally sets things into motion. But what if I, Rick Hubbell, made the following declaration: "I declare tomorrow to be a national day to honor my wife, and everyone will send her a gift." No one would expect a shower of presents to rain down from all across the nation. Yet if the President of the United States came on the air and said, "I declare that we are going to honor the death of a certain person by having a parade next Thursday, and we also encourage donations to her favorite causes." You can bet the tuba players would start practicing, and those charities would receive a flood of donations.

What's the difference? While my statement might have been well intended, it was irrelevant to your life. Besides, since I lack the authority to decree such a thing across this nation, it stood no chance of having the effect I wanted. On the other hand, the President's statement not only would strike a chord with people, it would be delivered by a person with the authority to declare such a thing; his decree would actually *set things in motion* as soon as it went forth.

In the same way, Goliaths will often not fall unless we make an appropriate decree.

I want to share with you four elements you will definitely need to deliver a game-changing spiritual decree like your ancestor's: (1) *Inspired Relevance*, (2) *Rightful Authority*, (3) *Deep Resonance*, & (4) *Supernatural Power*. (Please note: rather than go in-depth with this topic, I feel instructed by the Supremely Able Helper to only touch lightly on each element. He assures me that, for some reason, Giant Slayers will recognize the power hidden here, even if others race past.[7])

INSPIRED RELEVANCE

---

7 The Giants workbook available at www.tribofgiantslayers.com offers in depth study for those who would like to explore this more fully.

Inspired Relevance (Revelation)

Inspired relevance is having the wisdom of the Supremely Able Helper to know exactly the right thing to decree, at exactly the right time. In other words, the decree directly related to a given situation. You see, sometimes it's time to plant and sometimes to pluck; sometimes to search, sometimes to give up searching; sometimes to tear down, sometimes to build up. So what time is it right now? What exactly is the will of God for your particular situation, David? Our own logic, by itself, only gets us so far – even if we have renewed our minds by carefully studying the Inspired Guidebook. Often we still need to seek God to know His specific guidance for a specific matter.

Now in one sense, God's will is always in the Inspired Guidebook, but some situations require additional direction from Him. Let's face it, your Inspired Guidebook is filled with powerful statements which are all correct, all the time. Yet just because you close your eyes and randomly pick a verse, or even study out a topic, doesn't mean that any Giant in front of you will fall over dead simply because you recite what you see - even if you repeat it forcefully many times.

There is no replacement under the sun for the <u>particular</u> wisdom of the Supremely Able Helper for the <u>particular</u> situation you face RIGHT NOW.

Remember what your ancestor David proclaimed to Goliath? He didn't boast in his own strength or even God's, or simply quote some great truths from the Inspired Guidebook. David spoke something specific to the situation, a decree that the Lord put in his mind to say:

> "I come against you in the name of the LORD Almighty, the God of the armies of Israel, whom you have defied. This day the LORD will deliver you into my hands, and I will strike you down and cut off your head." *1 Samuel 17: 45-46 NIV*

When it comes to issuing effective spiritual decrees to slay Giants, you need more than a general idea: you need specific leading, David. You need to know exactly which passages relate to your current battle, and often other details as well; in other words, you need the inspiration of the Supremely Able Helper. Practically, this can be as simple as when you spend time reading your Guidebook: if one passage stands out to you, then pause. Don't just continue reading: wait there and listen for more instruction; mull it over. Believe that what you're reading has come alive in your heart for a reason. Maybe the Supremely Able Helper is trying to tell you something: ask Him.

Rightful Authority

For Giant Slayers, *Rightful Authority* ultimately comes from God. Having authority gives one the right to act a certain way in a particular sphere. For example, if I were a city police officer in the U.S., that would give me certain rights and expectations in a particular place. If you were driving down the road in my city and I flipped my siren and flashed my lights at you, I would expect you to acknowledge my authority and pull over. If you indeed recognized the law of the land and my place to enforce it, if you recognized my authority, then you would defer to it and stop. However, if I headed to NASA with my badge, and flashed it in an attempt to board the next space flight, I would undoubtedly be stopped by the security guards; there's no way they would let me through. My police badge, while hopefully respected, would not get me on a space flight because that isn't the sphere in which I had rightful authority. The astronauts there would have trained for years to fly on that mission, so they would be authorized for it, but not me.

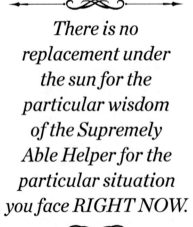

There is no replacement under the sun for the particular wisdom of the Supremely Able Helper for the particular situation you face RIGHT NOW.

In the same way, David, your True Identity and Special Assignment are sources of authority in the Spiritual realm. You might think of yourself as a pretty ordinary person, but when God calls you 'Mighty Warrior', and sends you to 'go in the strength you have and save Israel out of Midian's hand' as He did with Gideon - that instantly changes the game! **Suddenly, you have elevated status when it comes to fulfilling that certain Destiny, because God has now designated <u>you</u> as the person uniquely called to perform that task; you have been authorized by Him.** When God does the sending, the 'sent ones' enjoy His favor on that mission - and they are therefore much more fruitful.

The difference between 'sent ones' and 'goers in their own authority' is profound. When we are sent by God, we carry *His authority* with us! This is one of the many reasons to explore and know your True Identity and Special Assignment as best you can, David, as this knowledge will assist you hugely in accomplishing great things in life. (Unfortunately, far too many Kingdom citizens in the marketplace don't understand the importance of knowing and using their rightful authority.)

However, keep in mind that sometimes God chooses to confer authority on you through others – *not <u>only</u> directly from Him*. Even your great ancestor David - that great Giant Slayer - was actually *sent* into the battle to face Goliath by King Saul. The King was the one who told David "go"; he authorized the engagement. As full of Faith and slingshot Skills as David was, he didn't simply wake up one day and then decide to battle the Giant on his own initiative - he first sought the proper commission.

Also remember, David, as a child of God and a member of His royal family, you automatically and always have special status. You have become an ambassador of Heaven, which gives you particular rights everywhere on planet Earth: so you need to know what these rights are and how to use them. What gives you the right to stand up there and bellow at the beast? You need to know. The Supremely Able Helper, who will "guide you into all Truth", is extremely helpful in this area.

Battle Tip: Invoking the Name of the Lord

Let me give you one specific strategy concerning rightful authority that will serve you well in making decrees – and in fulfilling your Destiny.

Since the ultimate authority in every realm is the Lord's - *whatever you do, do it in the name of the Lord*. This should be obvious, but you would be surprised how many Kingdom citizens - who always operate at Base Camp in the name of the Lord - often forget to do so when outside it. For example, they may consider leading a small group or praying with someone at the altar as being 'the work of the Lord', but not business, holding political office, or serving on the school board; this is one serious miscalculation in life strategy!

> "And whatever you do in word or deed, do all in the name of the Lord Jesus, giving thanks to God the Father through Him." *Col 3:17 NKJV*

Despite many messages to the contrary, a Giant Slayer cannot separate the 'everyday world' from the spiritual one. All you and I do is in service to, and in the name of, the Lord. In every realm - whether parenting, surfing, doing business, writing movie scripts, spending time with your friends, feeding the hungry, preaching the gospel, or trying a case in court - everything belongs to Him.

DEEP RESONANCE

Deep Resonance (Firm Conviction)

I love this definition of 'resonance', from physics: *the state of a system in which an <u>abnormally large</u> <u>vibration</u> is produced in response to an external stimulus, occurring when the frequency of the stimulus is the same, or nearly the same, as the natural vibration frequency of the system.*[8]

How can this help you fashion a decree? Here's how. Resonance is when your life aligns with the way God has called you, David, and how He sees you. When this happens, you will 'resonate' with purpose and truth: Truth will bear witness of you and through you. **The resonance**

---

8 Dictionary.com

we're talking about happens when God's specific will, and His truths in the Inspired Guidebook, so merge into who you are and what you believe that they produce a greatly magnified effect in you. Jesus was so resonant with the Father that He could say things like "if you have seen me you have seen the Father," "not my will, but Your will be done," and "I only do what I see My Father doing." That's complete alignment; total resonance.

To decree something effectively, as Jesus and the apostles did, your decree must be born out of your resonance with the Father just as theirs was; it cannot just be something you happened to read once or twice, heard a sermon on, and then thought about for a minute. You might call this mixing the Word with Faith, or you could call it renewing your mind so completely that you resonate with the Truth. Such deep resonance is forged only in personal relationship with God. It usually requires extended periods of quality time with Him, meditating on the Inspired Guidebook, savoring and digesting its truths until they become part of you. Then when you speak out a decree, David, instead of merely parroting someone else, you will be speaking out an extension of who you are – and who He is. You will 'resonate' with the Truth. A parrot can't do that.

The process of forging such resonance isn't fancy, and it takes time, so too often would-be Giant Slayers skip this part – but it is vital. It takes spiritual maturity to recognize the need for this resonance and so put in the effort to achieve it, which is why the words of some Kingdom citizens seem empty, while others charge the atmosphere and change situations; it's why the mountain does or doesn't move.

But once you have achieved a level of resonance with Him, David, and you find yourself speaking to a Giant what He has told you to say, then – just as Moses, and your ancestor David, and many other Giant Slayers (and many Giants!) have discovered – that Giant is coming down!

187

SUPERNATURAL POWER

Supernatural Power

You can have the specific leading of the Lord (Inspired Relevance), elevated status (Rightful Authority), and even have taken the time to get as fully in tune with God as you know how (Deep Resonance) – yet still lack one thing that will limit your decree: Supernatural Power.

As a police officer, a badge is a great asset and symbol of authority. But at times you also need an *actual gun* or you will be in grave danger. Fortunately, our God is not short on power, even though frequently we seem to be. How can you and I attract more of His? The Inspired Guidebook is pretty clear that a condition may exist in our lives where we are like "clouds without rain"; talkers with little *demonstration*. In other words, just parrots. And that's a condition you definitely want to avoid. But if you find yourself lacking power, David, all is not lost.

The Supremely Able Helper is the one who carries the power of God through our lives. As human beings, we have a certain measure of power which has been entrusted to us: certain things are indeed 'within our power'. But far greater power is available to us through the Supremely Able Helper. To defeat Goliaths and accomplish great things, we need to learn to walk in step with Him, to be aware of His presence and leading in the everyday world. We need to get comfortable operating in situations beyond our control: situations which require far more than we could hope to accomplish by ourselves.

Inspired declaration at timely moments can turn the tables on what would otherwise be impossible.

But of course the greatest supernatural power comes from God. Once again - advantage, Kingdom Citizens! So let's learn more about this. As we continue on in later sections, we'll look more in depth at how to access Heavenly possibilities to meet Earthly needs; however, here's a valuable key.

Using Your 'Mouthbone'

To sum up, many Kingdom Citizens have not learned how to connect their 'heartbone' to their 'mouthbone': a simple disconnect that keeps their Destiny just out of reach. *I know it might sound crazy, but inspired declaration at timely moments can turn the tables on what would otherwise be impossible.* Along the Road of Destiny, sometimes you come up to an obstacle so great that the only way through it is to combine action with declaration. Making inspired decrees will increase the flow of 'heavenly possibilities' through your life.

Look at one example, the stunning supernatural reality of salvation. It's a promise from God that, while *available* to all, remains out of reach until two things are combined. Only certain people bring that promise of salvation from 'somewhere out there' right down into their lives. How do they do this? *They connect the promise they believe with a declaration*. They connect their heart and mouth.

> "...If you confess with your mouth that Jesus is Lord and believe in your heart that God raised him from the dead, you will be saved. For it is by believing in your heart that you are made right with God, and it is by confessing with your mouth that you are saved." *Rom. 10:9-11 NLT*

David, this is a mysterious secret that I urge you to explore more fully. In the same way the promise of salvation is accessed (by believing and declaring), a Kingdom citizen can bring other seemingly impossible things out of the realm of Heaven. This is one of the ways things move from Heavenly possibility to Earthly reality, one of the keys to accessing supernatural power.

Fashioning an Inspired Decree is *a matter of bringing Heaven's perspective into an earthly realm or territory, thereby effecting a thing's release.*[9] If you are going to slay a real Goliath, you will definitely need

---

9 To explore decrees more fully, check out the Giants workbook at www.tribeofgiantslayers.com.

supernatural assistance. One vital way to get this assistance is to harness the power of decree by learning to combine (1) Inspired Relevance, (2) Rightful Authority, (3) Deep Resonance, & (4) Supernatural Power.

Chapter 13

Key Takeaways & Giant Slayer Tips

- What comes **out of your mouth** often affects how situations turn out.
- A decree is an authoritative proclamation, which **in itself carries power to accomplish** something. A decree sets things in motion.
- **No parrots** allowed. There is more to releasing an Inspired Decree than memorization and repetition.
- To release an Inspired Decree requires: (1) **Inspired Relevance** (Revelation), (2) **Rightful Authority,** (3) **Deep Resonance** (Firm Conviction), and (4) **Supernatural Power.**
- **Learn to connect** your 'heartbone' to your 'mouthbone'.
- Fashioning an Inspired Decree is a matter of **bringing Heaven's perspective into an earthly realm** or territory, thereby affecting the Earthly reality.

Prayer to Defeat Goliaths

Heavenly Father,

What a privilege to walk the earth and champion Your causes; we receive Grace for every step. What an honor to have a Special Assignment straight from the King.

Help us to learn to Pray effectively, to step up with Courage when we should, to sharpen our Skills, and to employ Unconventional Tactics as You direct us. Show us how to combine spiritual and natural things to produce phenomenal outcomes that point people toward You and bring restoration in this world. Help us Focus daily on what is most important - to You.

Open our hearts to recognize Giants in the Land, and confirm exactly which battles we should fight and which ones not to. As we step out, help us choose the right Smooth Stones, and help guide each Stone to its target.

As we stare into the eyes of fierce Giants who would certainly defeat us were it not for Your powerful aid, give us the Faith and Courage to not back down one inch; shape us into Champions who bring improbable breakthroughs where You desire. Thank you for sending Your Supremely Able Helper so that we may accomplish what would otherwise be impossible.

Grant us the Hearts of Giant Slayers.

And in the everyday world, help us become more spiritually alert so that we are never caught off guard by the tactics of evil, but instead are always sensitive to Your Presence. We ask You to consistently demolish all wicked schemes against us. Protect us and those we love completely, hiding us in Christ, as only You can.

Use our actions to shake the foundations of the enemy's strongholds in our society, to free others from injustice, and even, we boldly ask, to alter the course of human history.

We dare to believe this, in the mighty Name of Jesus.

Amen

A Giant Slayer's Pocket Roadmap

To move forward into greater things, remembering how you got this far is immensely helpful. Below, review key points along the path and study the diagram. Look to the Supremely Able Helper for True Clarity. For some Giant Slayers this may be a great "Aha!" moment. As you read, allow yourself the freedom to 'feel' each season in your life. See yourself moving forward and growing stronger through each experience; don't rush it.

THE BEGINNING You see for the first time there truly is a God and you are not Him, that He loves you and sent His Son to rescue you. You realize things are messed up without Him. So you ask Him to forgive you for everything you've ever done wrong, you welcome Him into your heart and you commit your life to Him. Bravo! Your Faith begins growing. You get involved with others and start attending regular gatherings at Base Camp. You learn to worship God, and His Message comes alive – in you. Though there are rough spots, you keep going.

RESPONSIBILITY What next? You take **Responsibility** for *your* decisions, *your* actions, and what's been entrusted to *you* in life, yet you also believe God for the ultimate outcome. This combination is a major step for you. If you ever blamed others for your situation, now you're done with that and prepared to do what is necessary on your part to advance. You now combine dreaming with responsibility and follow-through, in new ways. You realize that with God the possibilities are always incredible.

TRUE IDENTITY & SPECIAL ASSIGNMENT You appreciate that since a wonderful Creator made you, you should study His purpose in that, and you yearn for clues to your **True Identity**. What did He design you for, you wonder? Who has He made you to be? What makes you tick; what skills do you have; where can you make a difference? You seek God about what He called you to do, how He wired you. Also, what is His **Special Assignment** for you? Your shape provides clues to where you fit, your purpose in life. But that's only the beginning, and you keep moving forward despite not knowing all the details. You make amazing discoveries as you travel both paths and they eventually come together at a remarkable place: *The Great*

Entrance to Your Destiny. Awestruck, you walk through.

PARTNERSHIP WITH GOD You come to see that everything in life has a spiritual side. Whether you are called to work at Base Camp full-time or not, there is a great calling on your life and you have a Special Assignment straight from the King. God is involved in all of creation; every part. So you determine in your heart that the only way to fulfill your Special Assignment and accomplish truly great things in life is to **Partner with God** in all that you do. You firm that up with Him. That means no 'checking in and out' of your spirituality just on weekends, mainly while doing 'Base Camp' stuff or only when it's convenient. It means living an integrated life. You and God do everything together, not simply because He is present, but because you now share goals. You intentionally work toward things He has taught you to care about and you enjoy spending time with each other. You see great things begin to happen.

HEART OF A GIANT SLAYER Your heart grows closer with God's as you faithfully tend to what has been entrusted to you. As you walk with Him, your longing for His will increases. You become freer from desires that used to magnetize you, such as selfish ambition, excessive craving for security, the need to feel in control, love of money, an imbalanced quest for others' approval, unforgiveness toward those who hurt you, personal influence for the sake of power, pride, guilt, lust, an overly critical attitude, fear, and others. It takes time. But freedom from those things is not even the best part: spending time with Him becomes more precious to you. You genuinely start to see why He cares the way He does, and you begin to care more deeply too. This goes far beyond a performance thing. He's your Daddy, and a Great King, and you fall deeper in love with Him. You learn more about His ways and it becomes much easier to hear His direction. It's clear to you that you have been given a precious opportunity to make a difference on Earth, and that He placed you here right now for a reason. The ways of the Kingdom become your ways, inside and out, in whatever you set your hand to.

FOCUS & SMOOTH STONES With God's help, you recognize that there are Giants in the Land, harming and tyrannizing people, and that

God wants everyone to be free. The Giants have already been beaten by His Son, but they linger, making trouble. They can be evicted. You also want God's glory to be reflected in you, and you know that when He is truly with you, your missions succeed, which is part of His seal of approval on your life. This increases your confidence. So you pick a **Giant Target** and **Smooth Stone(s)** to launch at it. Your target is something you are passionate about, such as a major problem worth solving, or an area of life where ungodly forces seem to be winning. When you hit the chosen target, you know that others will also benefit. Your **Smooth Stone** is your specific way of going after the selected target. A Smooth Stone can be a business, a particular role, a mission, project, idea, venture, initiative, ministry, team, group, or any *tangible* means to move toward a goal. You choose your Smooth Stones very carefully. You come to see the spiritual dimension of your Smooth Stones, even though many of those Stones are seemingly ordinary things in the everyday world. You continue your Partnership with God, Slingshot in hand. And the Giant Slayer in you awakes.

SLINGSHOT PRINCIPLES (PRAYER, COURAGE, SKILL, and UNCONVENTIONAL TACTICS) You realize that launching your Smooth Stone properly will take practice, and that's where your Slingshot comes in. Though you might already have been using some of the Slingshot Principles, you become more intentional about putting them together. You mix Prayer, Courage, Skill, and Unconventional Tactics in different ways, seeking the Supremely Able Helper's advice as to the best combination for creating the most acceleration and momentum in whatever you're doing. You take on smaller challenges to practice, discovering that *The Slingshot Principles* have an uncanny way of leading you toward victory in your pursuits.

SLAYING THE GIANT Acting when the **TIMING** is right, and bellowing at the beast with an **INSPIRED DECREE,** you step up boldly and launch your Smooth Stone. And a Goliath falls!!!

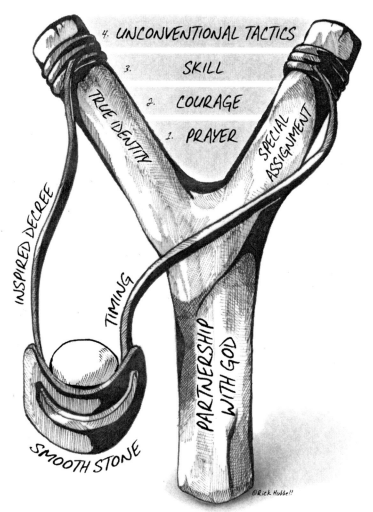

FOCUS

4. UNCONVENTIONAL TACTICS

3. SKILL

2. COURAGE

1. PRAYER

TRUE IDENTITY

SPECIAL ASSIGNMENT

INSPIRED DECREE

TIMING

PARTNERSHIP WITH GOD

SMOOTH STONE

©Rick Hubbell

HEART
OF A
GIANTSLAYER

SECTION III

Accomplishing Great Things in the Everyday World

Learn how to go beyond smaller successes to accomplish bigger dreams.
- Discover the Hidden Power of *The Slingshot Effect*
- Learn to Hear God More Clearly
- Become Skilled at Creating Strategic Alliances
- Learn to Overcome Several Kinds of Destiny Thieves
- Discover 10 Keys Giant Slayers Use to Change the World
- Step Into Your Destiny

It's right inside…

Chapter 14
As Giants Fall:
The Slingshot Effect

"... the people who know their God shall be strong, and carry out great exploits." *Dan. 11:32 NKJV*

So far, so good, David. We have explored how to Partner with God, and found a number of keys to defeating Goliaths. Yet in some ways, the greatest part of our adventure lies ahead. After all, finding a few keys to slaying Giants is not the same as <u>winning</u> the victories - let alone going on from them to do even greater things! And make no mistake about it: No matter what anyone tells you, or whatever stands in your way -- *you can accomplish great things.*

So what's the next step to put our new knowledge into action?

Well, let's watch a Giant fall. I want you, David, to actually see yourself

Make no mistake about it: No matter what anyone tells you, or whatever stands in your way -- you can accomplish great things.

slaying a Giant! Envision what it would be like to step up and defeat one. I mean right now: go ahead and picture it, in some detail. Dream a little; use your imagination; look with your heart. What kind of Smooth Stone would you choose? How would it feel? Who would benefit when it hits the mark? Picture the beast you want to slay, *and the result of seeing him fall.*

Surely a major breakthrough would result! Do you think you'd hear the words "Well done, David!" - and more than just a few times? I sure do! Everyone would be exclaiming: *"Congratulations, David! That was amazing! What Courage and Skill, the way you ran at that brute with just your Slingshot! Those crazy Unconventional Tactics were incredible! Most of us didn't think you stood a chance, but it's obvious that the Lord is truly with you in a way we didn't see before."*

To say the least, the onlookers would be stunned. Some would be reminding each other how you bellowed at the beast, making it known that *God* would deliver the ultimate victory - *before it even happened*; how your words seemed to drip with the heart of God and carry His intent. Your victory would not only demonstrate your great Faith, it would show that you really know how to Partner with Him and hear His direction.

And you'd be giving God the glory.

In your heart you would know it was a good thing that you learned to pray effectively and continued to communicate with the Supremely Able Helper in all you did. You might relish the thought of how you had grown even closer to Him through it all. What a feeling! You'd also remember how it felt as you moved into the fight, and how it seemed like you were clothed in *His* strength, not just yours. And in the moment when your Smooth Stone flew straight and true, accelerating unexpectedly, hitting the mark, sinking deep into the enemy - something would have forever changed.

Picture yourself on that battlefield, David, as the Giant falls. What would happen *in* those who were there? Concentrate. Don't you think such a victory would kindle a spark in them? After all, it's not every day that an unlikely hero conquers a fearsome Giant! Even though it was a one-on-one clash, the breakthrough wasn't yours alone, was it? As the Giant fell, can you picture how the Courage of others around you would soar, how *suddenly they would seem willing and able to do things they were previously afraid to try?* I mean if *you* could do something like that, they would begin to believe that *they* could advance, too.

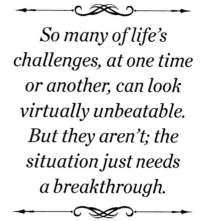

So many of life's challenges, at one time or another, can look virtually unbeatable. But they aren't; the situation just needs a breakthrough.

Yes, yes; exactly. When Giants fall, things change. Remember the Giants I encountered on my way to that city-wide planning meeting? Imagine how different that city would be today, if I had been able to slay several of those Giants right then and there? Even today, people would still be amazed at how different their city had become.

So what will happen in your life, David, when you slay a Giant?

Here is one of the mysteries of the Slingshot I don't fully understand, but will introduce here. An effective Slingshot attack involves the power of two amazing forces: (1) *Surprising Acceleration,* and (2) *Shared Momentum.* In the right circumstances these two factors are clothed with power from the Supremely Able Helper. In fact, no matter what Giant you face, these come in handy. The combination of these forces can be life-changing; I've named it *The Slingshot Effect.*[10] Let's consider this *Slingshot Effect* for just a moment. How do these forces work? What's so special about them? What does this really mean?

1. Surprising Acceleration often leads directly to breakthrough.
2. Shared Momentum enlarges that breakthrough.

---

10 (A new book called *The Slingshot Effect,* in the works, is based on case studies of people and organizations using the Slingshot Principles.)

The Power of Surprising Acceleration

Are you trying to accomplish something, and are in need of breakthrough? Would you like to start a new company, plant a church where most have failed, solve a problem society faces, lead a city through economic crisis, form a non-profit organization, develop an invention, create educational reform, or simply see the dream in your heart come to fruition? So many of life's challenges, at one time or another, can look virtually unbeatable. But they aren't; the situation just needs a breakthrough.

Listen closely then. When a well-chosen Smooth Stone is launched properly and accelerates toward its target, striking its goal - that involves <u>Surprising Acceleration</u>. When other people around become energized by the ensuing victory, this creates an additional surge of its own - that's <u>Shared Momentum</u>. Properly combining the Slingshot Principles produces this *Slingshot Effect*, one of the mysteries of this book.

Imagine being able to put these forces to work in your everyday life, David - and more than once. If you're a business owner, for example, a Surprising Acceleration in sales (provided your profit margins and fulfillment are ready) would make a big difference to your company, wouldn't it? Or if you are running for public office, a Surprising Acceleration in popularity near voting time would come in handy. Or if you are trying to increase awareness and support of a certain issue through a non-profit initiative, a Surprising Acceleration of strong new interest would help. Picture what would happen if you could harness these forces – and repeatedly!

<u>Surprising Acceleration can be especially valuable when others are competing against you; it has a way of catching them off guard and tipping the outcome your way.</u> While your sudden advance may not completely surprise you (because of your preparation that others haven't seen), it catches most people off guard. How many onlookers do you think really expected your ancestor David to beat the original Goliath? VERY few. *A surprising acceleration also delivers extraordinary impact.*

Shared Momentum

But the Slingshot Effect is not just Surprising Acceleration, it's also Shared Momentum: the combination is what delivers the greatest effect. But what kind of momentum, and who is it shared by?

To answer that, remember where we were just a moment ago. You were watching the Giant fall; you had started to imagine what would happen as he hit the ground, and you looked to see how others present would respond. You may have noticed how they suddenly seemed empowered to move forward. Winning an unlikely victory with God's help paves the way for more such victories: not just for you, but also for others. That's the mysterious power of Shared Momentum.

Here's another example. Have you ever watched a sporting event where one team is so hopelessly behind that even loyal fans head to the exits early? I'm talking about where the odds of a comeback are so low that even wishful thinkers have given up.

Recently I watched an NHL hockey game where my favorite team was down three goals, with only about 13 minutes left. We appeared totally overmatched that night. (Scoring three goals at any time in hockey is a memorable accomplishment, but when the game is on the line and not much time is left, it's nearly impossible.) In fact, *never in my team's history* had they come back to win a game when they were down by three goals late in the third period.

I like to avoid seeing the bitter end of a game in which my team is clearly out of it, so I was just about to turn off the TV - when we scored. It was just one goal, but it went in; a pretty nice one too. Too bad it was so late in the game, I thought. But then I noticed something peculiar: despite the very long odds against any form of a comeback, the rest of the team suddenly seemed to be skating better and playing a little harder - even though they all knew that their time was running out. So I stayed.

All of a sudden, just moments later, we scored again. Imagine that! Now we were only down one goal - and with almost five minutes to play! Could it be that we could come all the way back, not just to tie, but to actually win a game that just minutes before we had been sure to lose?!

As you've probably guessed, we did score again, and then went on to win the game in overtime. What a hockey game! That is still one of the most incredible momentum shifts I have ever seen.

So what happened?

One person's breakthrough - one goal - led to an even larger objective being reached and experienced by the entire group: a team comeback and a great victory. You see, David, often smaller breakthroughs lead to larger ones. People who discover and remember this truth can beat impossible odds time and again.

The Slingshot Effect works much the same way. When you successfully rise to an important strategic challenge, those who witness your victory often begin to mysteriously experience an increase in their own confidence. That's the power of Shared Momentum: it can prove highly useful in accomplishing great things in the everyday world.

Thinking Bigger than Goliath

Now the even larger question I have for you, David, is this: *Suppose you apply principles in this book, witness Surprising Acceleration, and a Giant indeed falls. What then?* **Would you retire to less dangerous pursuits after your big accomplishment, live comfortably off those rewards, and watch the others go on ahead? Or would you lead the next charge too, leveraging it into a rallying point for an entire group?**

After all, beating a Giant is only one exploit, and surely there would be more to do after that. The Inspired Guidebook says that "those who know their God shall do great exploits," plural. Jesus also said that we would do greater things with the help of the Supremely Able Helper. That's more than one exploit!

My point, David, is that what lies ahead of you in life requires both the willingness to slay Goliaths, as well as the fortitude to intentionally lead others into great victories of their own. To serve God and others honorably - to "love them as you love yourself" - you need to not only step up with Courage to wield your *own* Slingshot effectively and win a key battle or two, but continue to lead and manage well the part of

His Kingdom that the King has entrusted to you.

Why do certain people go from one great victory to more, while others have trouble winning just one - or else they let one notable success go straight to their head? *Those who accomplish great things find ways to overcome seemingly impossible odds - not just once - but time and again.* How do they do it? What do they know that most people don't?

One principle they understand is this: *A single, major victory is exciting, but multiple triumphs strung together produce truly great accomplishment.* These victors set their heart on running the entire race well, not just part of it. And Kingdom citizens like you, David, having the King's authority and the Supremely Able Helper available, are capable of not just one breakthrough, but many, so you've got to think bigger than just Goliath. A leader who others want to follow keeps forging ahead.

> "... the people who know their God shall be strong, and carry out great exploits." *Dan. 11:32 NKJV*

Aha, there it is: *"great exploits."* Let that ring true in your mind, David: say it out loud; repeat it. Go ahead and do it right now! That feels good, doesn't it? And David, it's one hundred percent okay to aspire to accomplish great things. The idea is that God's people will be filled with Courage to accomplish important things. That's YOU, David. That's YOU knowing God and finding Courage to act boldly, Courage to make a difference in the everyday world. That's YOU - not just defeating one Goliath, but going on to greater victories. YOU shall be strong and carry out great exploits!

If you move ahead of God and dream alone, before your heart is right and your motives have been tested, you will likely be driven by the dream instead of led by the Supremely Able Helper.

Now I know that many Kingdom citizens have been taught that pursuing an extraordinary life and achieving great exploits is only a matter of pride. The tricky part is they are frequently right. Let me explain; pay close attention.

When you are trying to accomplishing great things, there is another potent force also at work, but this one is trying to poison your noble intent, David. It's a sinister force called *selfish ambition*. Don't let it wrap you up! The good news is that one of the best antidotes to selfish ambition is something we've been working hard at achieving: knowing your True Identity and Special Assignment, and Partnering with God. Dream *with* God, not just on your own.

A word of caution: *Until your heart aligns and thrills with God's purpose for you, you <u>will</u> tend to dream mostly from selfish ambition; we all do. But you should know something: that road leads to an awkward, messy, dead end.*

But aspiring to do great things doesn't have to be selfish at all. As you partner with God in dreams that He inspires, *you will accomplish great things.* Like a tuning fork struck well, you'll make an unmistakable sound that attracts others and positively impacts their lives.

That's why it's critical to know your God. As you get to know Him, really know Him, He sorts out all these issues for you. Besides, you don't need to do everything perfectly, otherwise none of us would get anywhere. But if you try to move ahead of God and dream alone, before your heart is right and your motives have been tested, you will likely be *driven* by the dream instead of *led* by the Supremely Able Helper. Such is the unfortunate condition of many.

But if you'll allow God to touch your heart in its depths and transform you with His love, if you'll work at His pace for His purposes, then rather than achieving ultimately empty and unfulfilling goals, you'll find yourself dreaming about and achieving amazing things: important things; BIG things. Dreams sparked by Love and Faith; goals that align with your design and calling; wonders that God has placed deep inside your heart.

Let these words encourage your dreams of Destiny, David. They are exactly what I am praying for you now:

> **"With this in mind, we constantly pray for you, that our God may make you worthy of his calling, and that by his power he may bring to**

fruition your every desire for goodness and your every deed prompted by faith." *1 Th. 1:11 NIV*

That's right, David, let *those* dreams well up in you, right this minute: dreams of the profound difference that *you* can make in this world. Despite what you might have been told or have believed about yourself, it's okay to dream of going after life in a big way - when your desires spring from Faith in God, and from His desires for you.

Also, accomplishing great things is not necessarily about what other people think is great. It's about fulfilling *your* Special Assignment in light of what is possible for you in the grace of God. Accomplishing great things is about making the most of the opportunities and talents that God has given you. It has far less to do with how you stack up to others and everything to do with what God has made you capable of; it's about what God says is great. These are the great things that God wants you to accomplish, David. And I believe you will.

Chapter 14

Key Takeaways & Giant Slayer Tips

- The Slingshot Effect is what happens when a **well-chosen Smooth Stone** is used together with the **Slingshot Principles**.

- There are two main forces involved: 1. **Surprising Acceleration** 2. **Shared Momentum**. The combined effect often produces breakthrough.

- What lies ahead of you requires both the willingness to slay Goliaths, as well as the fortitude to intentionally **lead others into great victories of their own**.

- **Selfish Ambition distorts** the Slingshot Effect.

- A single victory is exciting, but **multiple triumphs strung together** produce great accomplishment.

Chapter 15
Blowing the Trumpet

"**If the trumpet call can't be distinguished, will anyone show up for the battle?**" *1 Cor. 14:8 MSG*

So, David, you are called to do great things, daring exploits. You aren't just imagining this, or merely *hoping* it's true: it is true! And you're on your way; new opportunities are all around you! But how will you enter into them? How can you keep moving forward from one breakthrough to the next? What actions can you take next that will lead to greater things? What steps should you avoid? When is it time to stop planning and begin to move out?

And how can you help others advance in their lives? After all, personal triumphs are wonderful, but the greatest achievements also involve lifting others. Long-lasting achievements usually require a team of people to sustain them. You need to see yourself as one who shines a light for others to follow, David, just like your ancient ancestor - and God's people need leaders. *Can you develop into the leader you are capable of becoming?* This will require a new level of Leadership from you. After all, what's in front of you, you've never done before.

What Is It?

All these questions demand one vital quality from you. And despite many brilliant works on the subject of personal growth, you rarely hear about this one.

Everyone needs this quality, David, but few have it. It can't be bought, but it can be obtained. Even when you have some, you still need more. You can't control it, but it can control you. Sometimes it's quite hard to find, yet it might be right in front of you. Once you have it, it can't be taken from you. When it's present, people sense it; when it's not, they disappear. It's not Wisdom alone, but it comes from Wisdom. All the Vision in the world can't replace it, yet it's essential for making worthwhile Visions come to pass. And it's something you probably don't possess nearly as much of as you think you do. To turn your Vision into reality, you need *True Clarity*.

True Clarity

You must be able to *see* clearly, *think* clearly, and - most importantly - *hear from God* clearly. You will need a clear understanding of your True Identity and Special Assignment, a clear understanding of where you are headed, and a clear understanding of what is truly important to you. This doesn't mean there won't be changes to the plan as you move forward. You need to stay flexible; but you must set out in a specific direction.

As a leader, David, you must also be able to *act* and *speak* clearly. People need to clearly know your expectations of them, and you need to know theirs. Leaders who are unclear can be brilliant, brave, lovable, and committed, but they are still hard to follow. Unclear words and actions send mixed signals, confusing people. If you had to take a train to a particular destination but weren't sure which train was the correct one, and if the conductor couldn't clearly answer your question, or if he told you he wasn't sure exactly where he felt like stopping that day, my guess is you'd want to choose a different train and a different conductor! **If you want to lead, people will be more willing to climb on board with you if they have some idea where you are headed.**

I'm not talking about the partial clarity that we can sometimes achieve on our own: so often we think we see clearly when we don't. Have you ever sped past a 'lack of clarity' warning sign, thinking it was no big deal, that you could just keep going and things would work out all right? I sure have: like the time I hit the 'Send' button on that email I wrote while angry and hurt. I thought my 'brilliant' response would put things in perspective for that other person, but boy, was I wrong! Now I wish I'd listened to that still, small voice that warned me not to send it. I should have left the pin in that little digital hand grenade, then disposed of it. I thought I was thinking so clearly, but my emotions tricked me: I didn't have True Clarity.

> "Those who follow me will never walk in darkness, but will have the light of life." *John 8:12*

What we all need in life, David, is True Clarity, and this comes from God alone: the clear truth about your Special Assignment and His specific directions for you; the clear truth about how others perceive you, about their motives - and about *your own*. Frequently, a lack of clarity is a clear sign that we need to ask God for His guidance.

God has told us in His Inspired Guidebook that by ourselves, in this life, we will never see things completely clearly, because without Him we are walking in darkness. Fortunately for us, God is always able to shine the clear light of truth into even our murkiest problems. And also fortunately for us, He can do this when we don't even realize that we <u>have</u> a problem! Like the time I learned more about True Clarity than I bargained for...

A Very Painful Lesson

It had been a busy day. Exhausted, I finally fell asleep. But my soft pillow couldn't lessen the blow of what I was about to experience, as I found myself in a vivid, life-like dream. In this dream, I was staring into dozens of TV cameras, squinting into glaring spotlights, and surrounded by a crowd of reporters sticking microphones into my face and all loudly bombarding me with questions. The noise was so great, I could barely make out their individual voices. I was completely overwhelmed by commotion. I just wanted to escape, so I turned to leave.

Just then, inside my heart, a voice cut through the chaos:

"Rick, I want you to have more influence. I've designed you for it. But you aren't ready."

Not ready?!!? How could this be? I was stunned. Now, I was humble enough to admit that I might not be ready for overwhelming media attention, but I was *certain* I could handle being more *influential*. Being told that I wasn't ready for influence offended me deeply, because I felt I had been doing all I could to move forward in life, taking all the right steps to prepare myself for the future. Sure, I'd had some setbacks, but I wasn't letting them stop me: I was working hard and marching bravely onward, doing my best to 'be all I could be'.

"What do you mean I'm not ready," I (in my mind) indignantly demanded of the voice. I was still trying to recover from the first major blow to my ego, but the voice's next statement *really* shook me.

"If I gave you a thousand people who would listen to you....what would you tell them?"

As the voice asked me this question, I suddenly found myself (in the dream) on the stage of a large, darkened auditorium, completely filled with people. The spotlights were again all focused on me, so I had to squint my eyes to see the faces of my audience. Each person was looking and listening intently, eager to hear the important words I had to say.

In my mind I proudly answered the voice: "I'm glad you asked me what I'd tell a thousand people, because I've been a consultant to companies all around the world! I've led dozens of workshops and classes; I've created many training materials and lessons; I've spoken to large audiences many times. So *allow me* to draw on some of my experiences!"

My mouth opened as if the first word of my speech was forming on the tip of my tongue. But instead of speaking, I just stood there, my mouth open, unable to think of <u>anything</u> to say. All my years of experience, all the wisdom I had gained, all the other talks I'd given: all had completely vanished from my mind, leaving me absolutely and embarrassingly speechless. I could recall <u>nothing</u>. And it wasn't a fear of public speaking that silenced me, because even in the dream I could remember having confidently spoken to groups like this many times before. But now I simply could not think of a single, solitary word to say; my mind was terrifyingly blank.

Stunned - and terribly embarrassed - I desperately searched my mind for *anything* worth sharing with my expectant audience.

Realizing that the voice belonged to someone important and spiritual, I guessed that its owner would be impressed if I shared the Gospel. 'Maybe that was God, somehow talking to me in the dream,' I thought. So, quickly composing myself, I shared a brief version of the Gospel with the crowd. It wasn't a great speech, but I hit the key points. In a few minutes I was finished; what a relief to have succeeded!

But the audience still sat there, waiting, wanting to hear more. Eager faces looked intently at me, begging for clear direction about something - anything. And I knew I should share more than just the Gospel, because after all, some of them, perhaps many, were already Christians. But I had nothing more.

Painful silence filled the auditorium. I felt as if I were drowning in it. Finally, totally humiliated, I simply left the stage.

Immediately, I woke up. "That *was* God," I thought, and "He's right. I'm <u>not</u> ready to do what He wants me to, and I don't know as much as I thought I did, even after all my 'accomplishments.'" This realization hurt me deeply: so deeply that I began to cry. The emotional pain so surprised me and so offended my pride that all I could do was wail. In the following days I couldn't bear to share my dream with anyone - but I thought about it all the time.

Eventually, in prayer one day, I mustered the courage to ask the Lord about it. Immediately I sensed the same voice from my dream.

"I'm not just talking about what you would tell them during a single speaking event, Rick," He said. *"If I gave you a thousand people who would <u>follow</u> you, where would you lead them? Where would they end up by listening to you?"*

I pondered the question for days, eventually concluding that I didn't have an answer. Why not?

…Because I wasn't aiming my life at a specific-enough target.

I realized then that I needed to *truly know* what I believe, what I stand for, and what I am called to do. Only then could I tell others why they should listen to me and why they should follow me, because only then could I tell them where they would end up. In other words, I needed True Clarity about my life and how I can best serve God and others; I needed to be able to see my life from God's perspective. This lesson was very painful to my ego, but it was a vital lesson for me, because God showed me that I was actually blind, when I would have told anyone who asked that I was seeing perfectly – and better than most people.

This is the kind of Clarity you also need, David, if you want to lead others on successful missions in life. True Clarity in leadership is like making a sound on a trumpet: *you must make a clear, certain sound if you expect anyone to follow.*

The Clarifying Process

After I finally understood the significance of my dream, I spent months clarifying what I truly believed and why it was important to me. I re-examined my motives and opened my heart to God. I listened intently for anything He might share with me - through others, as I read my Inspired Guidebook, as I prayed, as I went about my work. I wrote and rewrote personal mission statements, created flow charts, and penned diagrams – anything I could think of to help me clarify what I felt God was calling me to do with my life. This process has required countless hours and relentless prayer over several years – and I'm still pursuing it.

But the pursuit of True Clarity is worth every hour spent on it. It is directly connected to truly meaningful success in life. And since True Clarity comes only from God, we Kingdom citizens should have more of it than anyone else. And we can, David; just ask Him.

Chapter 15

Key Takeaways & Giant Slayer Tips

- True Clarity: **hearing from God** - and resolving to act in line with what He says.

- True Clarity sometimes comes at **special moments,** but also over time.

- True Clarity is **directly connected to meaningful achievement**.

- To **lead others effectively**, you must have True Clarity.

Chapter 16
The Importance of Strategic Alliances

"Though one may be overpowered, two can defend themselves. A cord of three strands is not quickly broken." *Eccl. 4:12 NIV*

Back when Solomon had this insight, a king's survival depended in part on regularly winning military conflicts. And when the lives of his people and the success of his kingdom are on the line, a *wise* king is always looking for the most strategic means to protect and advance his kingdom. While you are probably not in Solomon's exact situation today, David, his words still hold profound wisdom for accomplishing many great things. In fact, Solomon's wise words might be precisely what *you* need to surge ahead in life.

Let me paraphrase Solomon: *though you and I need to keep stepping up to the plate as individuals when it's our turn, properly aligned relationships (Strategic Alliances) will produce far greater strength than we could ever muster alone.* So go ahead and slay a Goliath yourself and enjoy the victory, David; you were indeed created to face certain such notable challenges by yourself. But flying solo *too often*, focusing on just what you can do in your *own* strength, will ironically <u>prevent</u> you from fulfilling your Destiny.

For many Kingdom citizens - even proven Giant Slayers - effective Strategic Alliances are what's missing. So if you're having trouble connecting the dots to your greater future, David, perhaps you are trying to accomplish something *alone* that instead requires the help of others. If this is so, how can you make it happen? Forming truly Strategic Alliances is not quite as simple as joining forces with whoever happens to be standing next to you, or generically asking others for help. You need to choose the right people to approach, and then align with them in proper fashion. This takes effort and wisdom.

Win/Win Scenarios

A Strategic Alliance is a pretty simple concept, actually: think of it as **a win/win relationship between two or more parties;** a relationship that makes possible something that otherwise isn't.

In a Strategic Alliance, parties provide something of value to the other(s). This added value can be complementary services, wisdom, access, compensation, trade, opportunity, protection, encouragement, shared risk, Faith, and more; *everyone should win.* (Some Alliances benefit one party more than the other, such as in a mentoring relationship; this is fine, as long as it's mutually understood and agreed on.)

<u>An important characteristic of Strategic Alliances is that the parties are independent.</u> In other words, *the bonds are formed with those NOT directly working for you or with you, but with people operating in other spheres of influence, and by and large independently from you.* So a Strategic Alliance is <u>not</u> a full partnership, for example.

To demystify this somewhat, let's look at one sort of Strategic Alliance quite prevalent in the music business. I recently bought an 11-song music CD. It's from a rising star who, in just a few years, has gone from being a relative unknown to popular the world over - and without the aid of "American Idol" or any other such major marketing gimmick. But 6 of the songs on the CD were co-produced with other artists. This is a form of Strategic Alliance.

Think about all the shared benefits when artists cooperate like this. First, each artist has their own audience. Some fans may follow both performers, but many follow only one or the other. By releasing a song together, each artist gets the shared benefit of access to the other artist's fans.

Win/Win.

But the possible synergies don't stop there. Think of other collaborative benefits: sometimes artists will also co-write a song, which gives it a flare and quality it wouldn't have had otherwise. Or think about the personal development possibilities of working closely with another artist and learning some new tricks, or meeting other skilled musicians whom you might work with on other projects. And the list goes on. The point is, it's no coincidence that the artist I'm referring to has had such uncommon success. In addition to developing Skill, this artist understands the value of Strategic Alliances.

Ponder this, David: in many cities across America, there are people with *as much or more individual talent* as that musician, but who will never gain a following. Many of them put all their energy into hoping to be miraculously 'discovered' one day, while walking right past opportunities to propel themselves - perhaps more slowly, but consistently - via strategic win/win relationships.

'Purpose-Driven®' Relationships

To say it another way: Strategic Alliances are 'purpose-driven'[11] relationships. *Some portion of the bond is aimed at an objective.* For some people, the idea of creating relational win/win scenarios for a purpose is distasteful: they think it's manipulative, 'political', or 'worldly'. If that's what you believe, you need to start thinking differently. Because *when you are truly going after what God has called you to*, there is every good

---

11 Registered trademark of Rick Warren

reason to work effectively with others – especially other Kingdom citizens - to achieve it.

I'll tell you what God calls believers who learn to build the right kind of Strategic Alliances, David: *shrewd*. And Kingdom citizens should be especially adept at forming alliances, since we have the Supremely Able Helper guiding us. (In fact, He has probably already prompted you to do this numerous times over the years, possibly even very recently. Have you learned to recognize when it's Him prompting you? Ask Him to help you do this.)

So you aren't a recording artist, and yet you want to know more about how to experience the power of Strategic Alliances? Fantastic! I'm certain there are possibilities right in front of you, or just around the corner which, if you learn to recognize them, can help you fulfill your Destiny. And who knows: while you're at it you might just help someone else do the same.

The Candidate Who Could Have Won

It might seem obvious that people who are more naturally relational would tend to have more effective Strategic Alliances, but that is not necessarily so. Having many relationships does not mean that those relationships are filled with effective Strategic Alliances. In fact, none may exist! However, it is true that it may be a tad easier for naturally relational people to find and form Strategic Alliances, due to them knowing and interacting with more people. Be that as it may, Strategic Alliances are possible - and essential to fulfilling Destiny! - for every personality type.

There are probably Strategic Alliances right in front of you, or just around the corner, which could help you fulfill your Destiny. And while you're at it, you might just help someone else do the same.

In a recent political campaign I observed the following: one candidate was attractive, charismatic, had previously held elected posts, and had lived locally for many years. As a result, she had a built-in support base that included elected officials, area business people, community groups, and long-standing friendships. She was outspoken about her Faith, held the same values that were important to many of the local constituents, and she even mentioned how God Himself had told her to run.

The other candidate was an older gentleman, a seasoned and respected leader who had a distinguished track record in law enforcement. He was also local, but had virtually no political experience, so he seemed like a long shot. Other than attracting those voters who wanted change simply for change's sake, he faced an uphill climb - but that didn't stop him from forging ahead.

As the campaign progressed it became clear that the race was tightening. Both candidates employed modest online efforts, signs, and other typical means of gaining votes.

But one Strategic Alliance in particular paid huge dividends. The political newcomer curried favor, and leveraged it highly, with the widely-read local newspaper. Story after story came out about the newcomer, with comparative silence or downright negativity about the other candidate. It didn't seem fair, but it was happening. On the night before the election, both the front and back pages of the paper featured the newcomer, who went on to defeat the well-liked younger candidate - and not just by a little, but by a resounding margin.

So what's the lesson here, David? Was God the cause of the defeat, and this was 'His will'? Perhaps, but I'm going to suggest another explanation. *A small number of highly Strategic Alliances usually outperform a large number of less strategic ones*, and in this case the less-experienced candidate was much more effective at identifying and building key Strategic Alliances to influence public opinion than the other. And in an election, influencing public opinion is what you must do to win.

Other factors of course played into the campaigns, but the alliance with the local paper arguably carried the election - and almost by itself; that *one* Strategic Alliance outperformed many less strategic ones. So while the 'favorite' candidate had many alliances, ultimately those all had little impact. She failed to identify and enter into the more valuable Strategic Alliances, so she lost - even though she was a phenomenal candidate and (quite possibly) obeying God by running.

David's & Solomon's Strategic Alliances

Both King David and his son Solomon realized the power of Strategic Alliances. Soon after slaying Goliath, David met Jonathan (King Saul's son), and they became instant friends; the text even says they loved each other like brothers. The two became such close friends, in fact, that they made a covenant with each other, and swore to always defend and uphold the other's best interests. *They went beyond mutual admiration and brotherly love into Strategic Alliance* – a Strategic Alliance which turned out to save David's life more than once!

Throughout David's life he formed many other alliances. And look how the value of Strategic Alliances was passed along between generations. After King David died and Solomon became king, you probably remember that the Lord came to Solomon in a dream and asked the new king what he wanted. Solomon asked for wisdom, to which the Lord said, "An excellent choice! And I'll also give you more than that."

Solomon was given exceedingly great wisdom, and one of the wisest things Solomon did was to set as a major objective of his life the building of a magnificent temple for the Lord. *So how did this very wise man, said to be wiser than any who ever lived, go about accomplishing such a difficult and years-long undertaking?* In 1Kings 5 you can read an important part of the story: <u>Solomon formed a Strategic Alliance</u> with Hiram, the King of Tyre. Hiram had exceptional wood in the cedars of Lebanon, and also men who were highly skilled in woodworking, and Solomon needed both for the temple. Hiram, on the other hand, needed wages for his men and food for the royal household.

A small number of highly Strategic Alliances usually outperform a large number of less strategic ones.

Very interestingly, the Inspired Guidebook says in this story, "The Lord gave Solomon wisdom, just as He had promised him." *In other words, the formation of this Strategic Alliance was itself an evidence of Solomon's wisdom.* So if the man said to be the wisest who ever lived used Strategic Alliances en route to arguably his greatest achievement, I think you and I, David, would do well to forge a few of our own.

Two Ways to View Alliances

So you can see how Strategic Alliances can generate outcomes that would be impossible by yourself. But how do you recognize the *right ones,* and harness their potential? One helpful way is to think about alliances in two basic categories: *Informal* and *Intentional.*

An **Informal Strategic Alliance** is a loose bond, where some unspecified level of good will exists. This could be as simple as an office receptionist who puts you (but not others) through to the boss; or a person you know who tends to refer you, and you them, when a referral is needed. *There are people you know, David, who are willing to go the extra mile for you on some level - whether or not you've ever specifically discussed it;* you can probably think of some of these people right now. These are Informal Strategic Alliances that you already possess.

Informal Strategic Alliances can be very helpful, such as one that recently produced a referral for me, which led to a major consulting project. But by their very nature, Informal Alliances are also somewhat unpredictable, because their terms are unspecified: so they usually only carry you so far. Such alliances rarely produce a specific, dependable, ongoing effect, and they can sometimes end abruptly. If you were a king whose country was being invaded by a vicious and powerful enemy, Informal Strategic Alliances with surrounding territories might result in you **not** receiving the aid you needed, when you needed it.

An **Intentional Strategic Alliance** is a bond which occurs as the result of one party seeking out the other - or a mutual exploration of synergy - which later becomes a clarified and specified win/win understanding. Intentional Alliances have more defined expectations than Informal ones, and they tend to produce more predictable results; they include a mutual and stated recognition of moving toward mutually beneficial goals. An example would be hiring a coach to help you through an important time in life, or you trading services with someone when launching a new enterprise. Having an Intentional Strategic Alliance means that you have more than a friend, you have an ally. Allies are useful; allies serve each other; allies help one another achieve things that would be impossible alone.

It takes both Informal and Intentional alliances to fulfill Destiny, David. And keep in mind, other people need alliances too – and some of those people are looking for someone like you. Sometimes relationships which begin as friendships become Informal Strategic Alliances, and then are changed into Intentional Strategic Alliances. And those may eventually develop past that stage and into some form of deeper partnership.

A Ceramic Adventure

My mother-in-law is a potter, and in the past she has collaborated with other potters. Not long ago, however, she found herself working alone. She continued to work at mastering her craft, but felt that something was missing.

All along, she had a very close friend who was also an exceptionally accomplished potter. For years they had been good friends who shared a mutual interest; they hadn't seriously considered mingling their pottery pursuits with their friendship, other than sharing a few words here and there. For one thing, her friend had for decades been focused on selling ceramics, while my mother-in-law was still growing her business from a hobby. Initially they were quite happy just being friends. As time went on, though, they began to exchange more ideas, provide encouragement, and talk shop. At that point, the friendship had also become an Informal Strategic Alliance.

Eventually these informal allies decided to explore synergies in a more specific way. They discussed a scenario where my mother-in-law would visit her friend's studio one day a week to help with the work, and in exchange she would get a closer look at how her friend operated so successfully. That's when their relationship became an Intentional Strategic Alliance. Her friend had a heart to help and mentor my mother-in-law, and my mother-in-law was a great source of encouragement to her friend. Win/win.

As you might imagine, as my mother-in-law helped out, her knowledge and confidence grew. As things progressed, her friend introduced her to other skilled potters. Now my mother-in-law has become far more successful at what she is doing, and she is now part of a prestigious, larger Strategic Alliance of potters.

The decision to move from friendship/Informal Strategic Alliance into an Intentional Strategic Alliance - and working together with someone else - was a little scary and humbling for my mother-in-law at first, but it has made all the difference in the world; it put her on a higher career trajectory. While not the only factor in her career advancement, it was certainly a key difference-maker.

Additional Pointers about Strategic Alliances

Some alliances are very short-term and are formed for one specific objective, such as when several groups synergize for a trade show; other alliances are long-term and deeper. For example, I have a friend of many years who is highly creative, a skilled graphic designer, and a gifted trend-spotter. Our families are also friends, but long ago he and I formed an Intentional Strategic Alliance. As a result of our alliance, both of us have benefited tremendously. Over the years we have helped one another achieve many things that neither of us could have done alone. For one thing, everything I do looks better and all he does sounds better; we frequently communicate about how we can serve each other, and what our expectations are.

One further tactical note about Strategic Alliances, David: It can be tremendously freeing to realize that you can be both strategic and helpful to others without you having to become consumed by <u>their</u> objective.

An Intentional Strategic Alliance is not a marriage, a full business partnership, or an abandonment of your unique Special Assignment. It's a limited-scope, mutually-beneficial agreement with many constructive variations to explore.

Remember, the alliances we are talking about are typically: a) between *independent* parties who are on (b) *distinct missions,* who collaborate c) *at some level* to create d) a win/win scenario for *both of them*. Alliance levels vary, so you needn't feel compelled to go beyond what makes sense. By clarifying expectations, you actually help each other more. Setting boundaries and clarifying objectives increases yield and avoids unnecessary conflict. And remember, David: the majority of your Alliances are better left Informal; choose your Intentional Strategic Alliances carefully.

A Noteworthy Base Camp Strategy

Here is one last incredible example of Strategic Alliances in action.

To varying degrees, most Base Camps (probably including yours) share the objective of reaching out to the poor, helping widows, and caring for orphans and the needy in the community. And of course there are also multiple non-profit organizations which share the same objectives. Many of these organizations hold quite similar values to the local Base Camps, and they have often been doing their charity work for many years: thus they are quite experienced, knowledgeable, and effective.

So you would think - with such powerful potential allies readily available and usually eager for assistance – that Base Camps would be working very tightly with their local charities, closely coordinating their efforts, and thus making a tremendous amount of headway with the local needs.

Far too frequently though, whether they intend to or not, Base Camps choose to operate so independently from any other Base Camp or local charity that the overall result in a given area is far below what is actually possible. Often, rather than sharing key resources such as expertise, manpower, or facilities, *Base Camps go after shared objectives largely alone.* For some reason, each one prefers its own special way of doing things over working together. While some occasionally join together for special events, they seldom collaborate in meaningful, ongoing ways.

But there's no reason it has to stay that way, David. To look at just one possibility, imagine the benefits if all the Base Camps in a town or county pooled their resources for helping each other's unemployed members find jobs, referring them to members of other Base Camps who need employees?

My own Base Camp is large enough that we could roll downtown in a caravan of cars, whip out our blow-up 'jumpy house' in a poor neighborhood to give the neighborhood kids an unexpected day of fun, while we handed out canned goods, tracts, and invited them to our Base Camp (which unfortunately would likely be too far away for their families to attend). We could also do a variety of other similar projects, but the big question is this: *what would happen the next day - and the weeks and months after that?* The likely answer is: *not very much.*

Sure, we could then invent our own special brand of assistance and try to sustain the momentum alone, but at our Base Camp we instead do something far more effective. Each year we choose several existing charitable organizations to be our designated Community Partners. These partners are not selected because they are affiliated with our Base Camp, but because they've demonstrated effectiveness at meeting particular needs, hold at least some shared values, and because they have needs that our members can assist with - and in person.

So instead of inventing our own mechanisms, thus having to re-invent the wheel, we support projects that people are already giving their lives to, thereby dramatically reducing duplication of efforts and other inefficiencies. We give regularly to these Community Partners and send volunteers consistently; we sometimes facilitate key meetings for these Partners and help raise community awareness about them.

The result is that these Community Partners are *freed up to focus more on meeting real needs,* and less on trying to raise funds and muster volunteers. There is profound wisdom in this simple arrangement.

Though there are other benefits to these Intentional Strategic Alliances, the real beneficiaries are the poor, the widows, orphans, and the needy.

Taking Initiative

Lastly, who is going to move first? You are. Yes you, David!

Take the initiative. Form that group you've been thinking about; meet with that person; explore possible synergies. Imagine the loss if Jonathan had said to David, "I think you're cool: let's be friends", and the two of them had simply left their relationship there. If they hadn't taken that further intentional step of forming an alliance, things might have turned out quite differently when Jonathan's father tried to kill David. *Just think of what would be possible in your life with a few well-chosen alliances.* Also, think of all the hurting, needy people in your community who could benefit so much from your Base Camp truly joining forces with other Base Camps and organizations. Think of all the Giants that would fall!

Whatever the great thing you are trying to accomplish, well-chosen Strategic Alliances can help you to win the victory. So you might need to sit down with someone, explore ideas, and hash out the details. You might have to take a risk and trust that person, group, or company. You might have to figure out how to turn a handful of your Informal Strategic Alliances into Intentional ones. OK, so not all your attempts will work out perfectly: that's life. But whatever amount of effort it takes, the investment will be worth it, because the right Strategic Alliance will radically change your life and powerfully advance the Kingdom.

Most important, Strategic Alliances and the synergy they produce are not 'worldly' concepts for Kingdom citizens to avoid: rather, they are God-given assets to fulfill Destiny, just as Jonathan was a God-given asset to your ancestor David.

So if you'll begin to apply what you've learned here, David – by recognizing the benefits of Informal Strategic Alliances and prayerfully considering where to form your next Intentional ones - you're bound to experience a surprising lift. Whether you find yourself just sort of 'stuck', or if you're yearning to accomplish some great things for the Kingdom but aren't sure how to make that happen, let me encourage you to prayerfully 'reach out and touch someone'. It can be as easy as contacting a wise, talented friend to meet for coffee, and asking how you can help each other – but that one simple step of fFaith could lead to an amazing future.

And never forget, David: you are already a partner in one vital Strategic Alliance, and a massively powerful one - your Strategic Alliance with the Supremely Able Helper. Your ally is always available with powerful encouragement and brilliant advice, He knows all the 'right people' and the best ways for you to connect with them, and His pledge to you in your alliance with Him is that He will guide you into *all truth*. (Ponder that truth for a while!)

All you have to do, David, is ask Him for direction and help.

Chapter 16

Key Takeaways & Giant Slayer Tips

- Strategic Alliance: *a win/win relationship between independent parties that makes possible something otherwise impossible. A relationship is a Strategic Alliance only if it is helpful in reaching an objective.*

- An **Informal Strategic Alliance** is a loose bond, where some level of unspecified good will exists.

- A small number of **highly strategic alliances** usually outperform a large number of less strategic ones. Therefore, *focus on potential high-yield alliances.*

- An **Intentional Strategic Alliance** results from one or both parties *intentionally seeking* a mutual exploration of synergy.

- When creating Intentional Strategic Alliances, **setting boundaries** and **clarifying objectives** increases the yield and **avoids unnecessary conflict.**

- **Changing an Informal Alliance to an Intentional one** can **sometimes** mean the difference between success and failure.

Chapter 17
Quitting & Other Destiny Thieves

"It's not that I've already reached the goal or have already completed the course. But I run to win that which Jesus Christ has already won for me." *Phil. 3:12 GWT*

Though I never enjoyed running for its own sake, I have always appreciated its value for conditioning. Growing up playing soccer, baseball, lacrosse, tennis, and racquetball, I quickly learned that running makes a big difference. But I wish it didn't.

Not being particularly fast, I huffed and puffed and held my own. Well, most of the time, anyway: sometimes people blew by me. In competitions I could occasionally find an extra gear at key moments that surprised my teammates and opponents, and even myself - a gear I rarely displayed during practice or warm-ups. But I simply didn't have much natural talent as a runner. So I had to work harder just to play at a reasonably high level. My rare, timely, adrenalin-fueled speed-bursts were kind of a mystery.

I realized that athletes who put time into running, regardless of their natural endurance and speed, tended to do things slightly better toward the end of a contest – when everything is on the line. Since I wanted to be a 'go to' guy, someone who made the difference when it mattered, I always tried to stay in pretty good shape.

Although I played sports all through the college, I never thought twice about trying to become a professional athlete, for obvious reasons. But I managed the talent I did have as best I could, and I was elected co-captain of my college varsity lacrosse team. Then college ended, and all the hours I'd put into sports over the years, which had taught me so many things, rapidly ran out of useful athletic outlets.

I was at a crossroads: one day there simply were no more teams to be on, other than softball teams and club leagues. So I started playing racquetball more intensely, and eventually won a few tournaments here and there. I didn't play consistently over the years, but I got pretty good. Still, there was that running thing.

One summer, in an effort to keep in shape, I started running at a nearby college track. Determined to stay in shape, I got into a groove and forced myself to train regularly; I began timing myself, always trying to go faster, which I frequently did. Striving for constant improvement was mentally and physically exhausting – especially doing it all alone. The funny part is, for me, it wasn't only about running. It became about life. Here's why I say that. One day, David – a day when I really, really felt like quitting - something important happened.

A Remarkable Finish

I was coming to the end of a couple of timed miles. This particular day, no one else was there but me, the hot tarmac, and the sun, laughing at me. As I rounded a corner, all the distances I'd put in over the entire summer, and the intensity of the training, seemed to suddenly pile up on me and overwhelm me, mentally *and* physically. "What am I doing here," I thought, "constantly pushing myself to go faster? Seriously, who am I kidding? I'm finished with this."

It wasn't that I wanted to quit running altogether. It's just that right then, in the final exhausting stretch, my fatigued body wanted to slow down and cruise to the finish instead of pushing. Hey, some days you just don't feel like it.

"No one sees me, and no one would care about me slowing down; no one," I reasoned with myself. "No one even cares if I run or not." But I kept looking at the clock as if I were still racing it. "Me and my little world," I thought. Then - totally unannounced - an idea dropped into my mind. It was just one tiny idea, but it was also a truth so powerful that it has never left me. And it has provided me more strength in trying times than I can begin to tell you, David. Here's what I heard:

"**Anyone can quit, but far fewer keep going**. Absolutely anyone in the entire world in your shoes right now could slow down. *Anyone.*"

It was true; not a soul on the planet would have a tough time choosing to ease into this finish. With no one else looking and no one else aware of my choice, who wouldn't just coast? Giving myself a break - a reward for all my hard work, you might say - would be so easy, and it seemed so obvious - and so harmless. Yet the more I thought about doing what not everybody could or would do – i.e., NOT slacking off, NOT quitting - the more it seemed to make sense. And I used those thoughts to encourage myself.

Struggling to keep my pace, since I'd already given in momentarily to the idea of slowing down, I tried to pick it back up a bit. Drawing strength from who knows where, I pressed harder, my lungs and legs burning. "If I want to be a difference-maker," I thought, "I must be willing to do some things differently than others." Though I had heard similar messages before, none had ever sunk in like this one. I pushed the pace.

"I need to keep going when they wouldn't. And in one sense, forget about *them*. I need to keep going when *I* feel like stopping. And all I have to do is choose. Otherwise, I'm taking a path that everyone else could. And where everyone else is going is not where I want to head. That's not running to win, that's jogging with the pack; that's quitting on the better possible future. But *not* giving in right now, when the stakes *aren't* high - that can help me in much bigger moments."

Knowing when *not to quit* can help you accomplish great things, David.

In fact, it can sometimes be the lone deciding factor between success and failure. I don't know what's been going on in your life lately, but are there places where you've been tempted to quit, that maybe you shouldn't? Are you certain that quitting would be the right decision? Sure, sometimes you make a mistake; then you see that you're headed for trouble, and you need to stop throwing good money after bad, so to speak. But what I'm telling you is *there are times when you may feel like giving up which hold keys to your future.* Better learn to make *sure* you can tell the difference between the time to quit and the time to press on. (Hint: Ask God!)

Lack of will to press on during moments of fatigue or discouragement is a common reason why some Giant Slayers never accomplish great things in life.

Other Destiny Thieves

There are also external forces that can stop your Destiny, David. Let's call them Destiny Thieves. Among others, beware of *unexpected knockdowns, letting money make your decisions,* and *people who can't envision your future.*

Unexpected Knockdowns

Sometimes a situation, a temptation, or even a Giant may get the better of you for a time. How you choose to respond - and it is always your choice, David - means everything.

When the flood comes in, it's so easy to forget where you were heading before it happened. Maybe you lose a loved one, a dear friend betrays you, an accident occurs, or an illness alters your life. Perhaps your business fails despite your Faith and hard work; you lose the election; or the important opportunity you were so looking forward to simply vanishes. Maybe the love of your life doesn't love you back. Perhaps you make a big mistake which hurts others, and you have trouble getting past it.

If you haven't had such a setback, David, hallelujah! But trust me, somewhere on your journey you will encounter one, so you would do well to listen to me now. Just making it through such a painful time is hard enough, as you might imagine - but rekindling your desire to accomplish great things can prove even more difficult. After such a traumatic experience, becoming discouraged will be a grave threat to your future. So be prepared to find a way through the storm; you must.

This happened to my family when our son passed away unexpectedly. That kind of loss can rip you completely apart,[12] but by the grace of God, for us it didn't; it was a defining moment and a tragic loss, but not the end of everything. My wife and I have met scores of people with God-given dreams who lost momentum when an unexpected event or a very bad decision rocked them – and who haven't regained it. We determined that we would not allow ourselves to fall into the trap of self-pity or despair. In fact, we chose our son's death to mark a new beginning, allowing the Lord to use our suffering to make us stronger, and we made that decision even before any of it made any sense.

That's why I am telling you this, David. No matter what happens, keep moving forward with God.

The Pot of Gold

Another Destiny Thief is the temptation of fame and fortune. Here's the story of a time I nearly fell prey to this thief.

A few years ago my wife and I were seeking God's will concerning an offer of employment I'd received which required a geographic move of thousands of miles. Neither one of us was at peace with this job offer, even though it seemed ideal in many ways: the position was solid, with a healthy salary, the job was within my skill set, and the company was in a beautiful area of the country not far from family. We had absolutely no obvious reason to feel uneasy about the offer, but we were, and no matter

---

12 For more, visit www.thestoryofnathan.com

how hard we tried and how much we prayed, we couldn't shake our lack of peace. So after a great visit to the company, I politely communicated that I didn't think a full-time position was for me, but perhaps I could do some consulting for them.

The company owner was quite persistent, though. He felt certain I was the right person for the job, and he wanted me full-time, so he invited my wife and me together for a second visit. Upon our arrival he whisked us to a delightful 5-star restaurant for lunch, he shared more about his vision for the company, and we had a great time.

Then he brought us back to his office and we talked further. I had already declined his initial offer and counter-proposed a consulting arrangement, so I didn't know exactly what else to say, but having my wife with me added a totally different dynamic. She could feel out the whole thing with me in person, and add her sense of the situation and the people, so I felt much more at ease. Plus, my wife is just plain wonderful and engaging, and most everything is more fun with her, so we were having a fantastic time.

Then the owner sprang a major - and quite flattering - surprise on me.

Instead of me becoming a vice-president, he now offered me the position of president of an entire division, with a higher base salary and even more benefits! This new offer really surprised me. Later that night, as my wife and I talked in our beautiful hotel room that looked out on an impressive atrium lobby, we imagined the possibilities. We talked about how we felt inside, then we prayed - and we decided to accept this new offer. The next morning we relayed the news and began the crazy logistical mayhem that accompanies these kinds of things: movers, real estate, schools, etc...

Now we didn't accept the offer purely for the money, David: we knew better than that. But we did feel that the increased offer was surely a sign of God's favor on it.

A few months into my new job, though, I began having significant inner turmoil. On the outside everything was still fantastic: the position and surroundings were great, and I had even recruited a friend to also relocate so he could work with me. But I began to struggle with the strategy of the company, as it appeared to me that the course the owner was committed to wasn't going to lead where he supposed it would. Being a bit of a strategist, I began to ask him about it, to see if any part of the plan could be modified.

Yet the owner did not want to change anything: not one single facet of his plan - and I do mean <u>nothing</u>! He dug in and reiterated in no uncertain terms exactly how things were to go. But I had to give him credit: up until then he had been quite successful, and he knew what he wanted.

Over the next few weeks, though, as I continued to ponder the matter in my heart and before God, I became increasingly concerned, and I had to make a difficult decision. I could stay and maintain the *status quo* (and my wife and family loved our new life), or I could listen to God's leading in my spirit, which was growing ever clearer.

But was it really the leading of the Supremely Able Helper, telling me to leave? After all, there were many things to like about the situation, and besides, we had only just arrived. And anyway, why would God lead us to such a dead end? That didn't make sense to me. As I continued my internal debate, more and more investors and high-powered business types entered the scene in various ways, all saying how much they loved the owner's plan. I continued to voice my opinion that unless the strategy was refined, the company was headed for trouble.

David, not one single co-worker agreed with me enough to also challenge the plan right then.

But I eventually came to the decision that the plan was indeed wrong, and so I knew that I had to move on. After all, it was the president's company, so he had the right to take it in whatever direction he wanted. After talking things through with my wife, I handed in a courteous but clear 30-day resignation notice - with no backup plan of any kind.

Everyone was stunned, including our friends and relatives. What were we going to do next? I didn't know. There was so much pressure to figure out something quickly, for obvious reasons, but I had no idea what to do. All I knew was that I had followed the Lord's leading, the best I knew how. I felt it was He who had led us there, so He would lead us out.

I decided to go to a remote cabin to pray for a while, hoping that I would receive a clear plan for what to do next. I prayed day and night for almost a week - and a strange thing happened.

Out of thin air, two new job opportunities came into view; and except that they both required relocation, these two choices were completely different. On the one hand, I felt a strong internal leading to *go and volunteer* to help develop an organization. This choice would not only require a move all the way back across the country – but I had never met the person I would be working under! On the other hand, a great job opportunity with a very high guaranteed salary (about twice what I had been making as president) had appeared – and the company was on the east coast, closer to where we were.

It was kind of miraculous, really, receiving these two clear options in answer to our prayers. But with all the expense and emotional exhaustion of moving that we had just been through, how could we put the family through all that yet again? Still, we had to decide, as no opportunities had opened up where we were. I thought that surely the position with financial security for my family must be the provision of the Lord. Yet deep in my heart of hearts, I instead began to feel increasingly certain that we were supposed to choose the volunteer effort.

My wife and I talked everything through, and we decided that volunteering, as crazy as it seemed - and not knowing for sure how we could handle it financially - was indeed the path of Destiny. Then, out of the blue, as we made our plans to move yet again, a deal that I had been working on for five years closed, and this provided the needed funds to make the volunteer effort possible. Without those proceeds there would have been no way we could have followed our hearts. But had we chosen the extremely high-paying job, I believe we would have left the path of Destiny. (That being said, that is by no means the case in every situation!) Making the 'crazy' choice turned out to be one of the best decisions we ever made. It is part of the reason I now have the opportunity to meet you through these pages, David.

Incidentally, within two years, the company I had resigned from - which seemingly had everything going for it when I left - fell apart completely, leaving behind a mess for all concerned. Only in the aftermath of the train wreck did a number of other former employees mention that they too had seen it coming. (Funny, where were they when I <u>first</u> proposed refining the game plan? Oh well, we all learned something!)

David, remember this: there is no cost too high and no challenge too great that it is worth leaving the Road of Destiny. Destiny Thieves will present themselves in many ways to get you to stray from it. Don't do it. And if you do happen to find yourself off the path one day, simply repent immediately and ask the Supremely Able Helper to show you the way from there; He always will.

Naysayers

There is one last Destiny Thief I want to mention (though there are others): the Naysayer. The Naysayer can be tricky to recognize, and often lurks surprisingly close. If his ideas penetrate your defenses, it will cost you.

On the one hand, you desperately need to listen to wise counsel; you cannot accomplish great things without it. Period. On the other hand, you <u>must avoid listening</u> to *people who cannot envision your future*, because if you don't, they will cause you to veer off course.

It would be simple if you could make two categories: Destiny Builders & Destiny Thieves. Hang out with Destiny Builders and avoid Destiny Thieves. At first, that may work to some degree; some types you can easily identify. You know people who don't encourage you toward your godly future. You also know a few people who encourage you. Add Builders, subtract Thieves. Use this basic equation to your advantage and it provides a lift in the right direction.

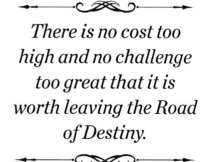

There is no cost too high and no challenge too great that it is worth leaving the Road of Destiny.

"*But is life really always that simple?*"

What do you do when someone brings a little of both, or you're dealing with a person who falls in the Destiny

Thief or Sometimes-Destiny-Thief category, and you can't just avoid them? What if some of the negative input comes from your mother-in-law, a key associate, a long time friend, or even a mentor or leader?

On the obvious decisions, David, I'm counting on you to nurture the right friendships and relationships. But in some of these other instances, it's a tougher call. You need to find a way to handle these situations without creating awkward tension or becoming discouraged.

This is the time to pause and pray for a second. Do you have to always state your case in every conversation, especially when someone is being aggressive toward you with their 'insight', which may be off-base? No. You don't. Wisdom is sometimes silent. Don't alienate others just because they can't see your potential the way you do, or because they have a way of 'pushing your buttons'. Neither should you give in to their way of thinking.

And anyway, how come some of these Naysayers are having more of an effect on you, David, than you are on them? Remember your Internal Compass, your Supremely Able Helper, and True Clarity? They must guide you.

The plot thickens: on occasion, God allows you to come to a place where others whom you respect and love don't believe in the direction that you think you are supposed to go. Sometimes He allows this precisely so you will learn to trust and obey Him above anyone else.

As important as it is to listen to input from others, David, it is critical to obey God above all.

When conflict comes between these two forces - and it will! - once you've weighed things out as best you can before the Lord, *your own sense* of God's direction is the one to go with. That sounds obvious, but let me make it even clearer. At the end of your life on earth, when you give account for the decisions you made and things you did, don't plan on saying, "Well, this is what so and so thought I should do." That won't fly. You won't be held accountable for what everyone else thought you should do, David. One opinion trumps the rest by a long shot: *His.* I'd rather look awkward trying to obey Him, and have people question me, than please everyone now and look awkward on Judgment Day. How about you?

So here is the sum of the matter. All the frequently cited examples of people who refused to quit, like Abraham Lincoln (after losing many elections), Truett Cathy (being told fast food restaurants not open on Sundays could never succeed), or Thomas Edison (completing 10,000 experiments without creating a viable light bulb), won't amount to anything for you - if YOU don't find resolve when YOU need it.

I'm not certain what will happen if you keep showing up, but I have a pretty good idea what will happen if you don't. So I want you to continue with what God has begun in your heart. If you've lost the Vision, pick it back up; if you've gotten tired, pray for strength. You know, David, whether you step up to fulfill your highest God-given potential or not, you will still have to face Destiny Thieves; everyone does. Since you have to fight battles anyway, while you're at it why not fight - and win - the important ones!

Chapter 17

Key Takeaways & Giant Slayer Tips

- ☑ **Destiny Thieves come in many forms** and can be hard to recognize.

- ☑ One of the greatest Destiny Thieves is quitting. **Anyone can quit**, but fewer can keep going. Simply **knowing when not to quit** can help you accomplish great things.

- ☑ Other especially deceptive thieves are **unexpected knockdowns**, the **lust for money or fame**, and '**helpful' advice** (that isn't so helpful) from people close to you.

- ☑ **Obey God.** Remain humble, teachable, open-minded, and charitable toward everyone, but you must always obey God over any person.

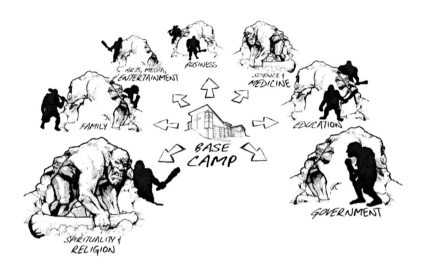

Launching Out

"...Your kingdom come, your will be done, on earth as it is in heaven."
Matt. 6:10 NIV

David, as our time together draws to a close, I want you to know something: *the honor has been mine,* and I have deeply enjoyed the privilege of spending time with you. So pardon me for feeling like today is bittersweet. Our journey together is coming to an end to make way for something greater: *Your Destiny.* That's what this is all about anyway.

Along the way, I trust you discovered more about how much God loves you and how truly great His plans are for your life. If not, I have completely failed you. And while my goal has always been to help *you* grow stronger - in the process of writing, I too have grown in many ways. Thank you for that.

You can't imagine how much I look forward to someday hearing about the part of your story which today is yet unwritten. To learn what you experience walking through the Great Entrance to Destiny and what you discover on the other side will be my delight. That you would dare to partner with God, defeat Goliaths, and accomplish great things in the everyday world is incredible, yet in my heart I clearly see you achieving these great victories.

I also envision this: that you and other new-generation leaders, from all walks of life, will use the *Slingshot Principles* and others to defeat Goliaths and pioneer fantastic advances around the world. You will change things - and in ways that will surprise you. As you do, dreams will be realized, resistance will crack, businesses will grow, ministries will thrive, breakthroughs will come, leaders will step up - and God will be glorified.

So go ahead - become a missionary as you have dreamt; build a great company; win that election; believe God for promotion; invent the cure; pioneer that prayer center; improve the schools; deliver the needed healing; write that book; champion a just cause; mentor those precious ones. Give generously, lay down your life, demonstrate the Good News - and slay Giants!

Always remember, David, all the mess in the world isn't something to avoid: it's an invitation - an invitation from God! The question is this: What are you and I going to do about those situations while we're here?

In our Base Camp meetings we often talk about right and wrong, and that can be eye-opening. It's also great when we declare what we believe, and pray for solutions. When we celebrate God's goodness together, it's life-changing. But by themselves, all of those things put together will not solve most Giant problems. *David, we also need to send in champions like you into the middle of the fight.*

While some Kingdom citizens wait by the bus stop and hope for God to get us out of here, that isn't the path for a Giant Slayer.

The world is waiting, looking for answers; it's wondering why it's here and what it's for. But the parts spinning out of control do have solutions. While the world's only hope is in God, on Earth He often works through His sons and daughters, and powerfully so.

The entire earth *does* belong to God, and He is raising up Giant

Slayers for every arena of life. This Tribe of Giant Slayers will display His greatness. They will carry the Good News in word and action, and their demonstration throughout the world will cause many to turn to Him.

Yet many of us miss our Special Assignment. Some simply never recognize theirs; others exchange their Special Assignment for something infinitely less valuable.

When this happens, answers that were supposed to show up don't arrive as God intended. Sure, He's got ways to make it all work out. But He has entrusted us with important missions, not insignificant ones. When you and I don't fulfill what we are capable of in Partnership with Him, planet Earth gets messier. *But when we do, everything changes - and in ways even beyond what we expected.* So the world needs you to fulfill that important Special Assignment that God has given to you, David!

Things Giant Slayers Can Do to Change the World

Now it's time to pass along one last treasure to you, David, to assist you in becoming the Difference-Maker you are capable of being. These 10 simple practices will change your life – and the world!

1. Seek the Kingdom of God First

Make what is important to God important to you; structure your life around this. Love Him and His priorities, and everything else will fall into place.

2. Honor People

Show respect and honor to everyone: weak or strong; rich or poor; spiritual or unspiritual; 'cool' or 'uncool'; big or little; expert or novice; like you and nothing like you. Make time for other people; listen to them, help and encourage them. Serve others and celebrate their accomplishments.

3. Dream B.I.G.

Dare to envision exploits. 'B' is for *beyond human ability*. Think beyond what you can do alone. 'I' is for *inspired by God*. Make sure the spark is from Him. 'G' is for *generation serving*. Reach out to change the situation that God has purposefully placed you in.

4. Stick to the Path

Discover and walk in your True Identity and Special Assignment: do not trade them for anything. Resist the temptation to blend in or try to be someone God never intended. Enjoy life, yet don't squander it. Challenge the status quo when necessary. Fulfill *your* Destiny. Never give in to Destiny Thieves.

5. Partner With God

With His help, you can defeat Goliaths and accomplish great things: truly great things. Get to know Him and learn to trust Him; enjoy the journey of building your relationship with Him. Invite Him closer than you ever have before; you can trust Him completely.

6. Lead by Example

Be a thought leader, a conduit of exceptional solutions, and a demonstrator of effective living. Get involved in making the Earth more Heavenly. Your life should carry an Unmistakable Imprint which points others to God. *It is easier to criticize than to lead, but don't take the easy way out.* Criticism by itself is the language of observers. So don't cast blame or criticism, instead show the better way to do things.

7. Get Sent

I recently had the privilege of leading a 9-week workshop called *Stepping into Your Destiny*, based on this book. One of the highpoints was when the faithful Leader of our Local Base Camp came to the last session to commission each participant into Destiny, launching us toward it. Being sent or commissioned (whatever that looks like in your situation) by someone with spiritual authority, releases something truly profound into your life.

8. Live by Faith

The promises of God are not automatic, so you must live by Faith. The journey often begins where the path seems to end. Pray and declare in such a way as to release Heaven's resources to meet Earth's needs. Call those things that appear not as though they are. Keep believing no matter what.

9. Slay Giants

Use the Slingshot Principles. Advance inspired projects. Fight injustice. Don't back down from Spiritual Giants or Giant Problems. Face the big things. Become a difference-maker right where you are. Allow the Supremely Able Helper to make possible what otherwise isn't - through *you*.

10. Spread This Message

If our time together has opened your heart to Destiny in any way, know that others are also waiting for guidance and encouragement. There are people, organizations, and Base Camps that may hear best if they hear from you. Responsive hearts are ready to listen in many places. Share strategically, and then watch what happens.

Walk Wisely & Work Together

As you launch out even more purposefully into the everyday world, David, know that every minute of every day, in every location (whether it seems 'spiritual' to you or not), belongs to your heavenly Father. And there are both natural and spiritual realities to everything. So combine spiritual belief with strategic action in all you do; keep both in mind at all times as best you can. Not doing so puts you in real danger.

With so many Giants at work in the everyday world, it energizes them when you forget to show up to work like you know you are on the Road of Destiny. When that happens, you lose advantages that God has provided to you. So Giants lick their chops - waiting for you to arrive half-armed, half-aware, and half-hearted. A Giant Slayer cannot afford to think like that.

As you ponder what we've discussed, remember this, David - probably only a few of the principles in this book apply to you right now. Focus on them first, and save the rest for later: in whatever combination and timing the Supremely Able Helper directs.

Let me also remind you that God has appointed special, dynamic leaders, who know Him well, to serve strategically in various positions: their insight and efforts are irreplaceable. Do not follow those who downplay the importance of these leaders. (Serve honorably if you are one of them.) Whatever your Assignment may be, always stay connected to Base Camp. But remember, David, not to focus your entire life within its walls unless that is your Special Assignment, since most Giants are out in the everyday world.

In the end, we all work together.

Go Forth

As I write these last words, I am filled with a sense of *your Destiny* in my heart. David, I firmly believe that now is the time for you to move ahead. As you look around and see the world's problems, though Giants have created many and humans have caused others, step up. Stand for justice. You carry solutions that the world is waiting for, so don't delay. Show others the Way.

God is interested in *all* creation. He sent His own Son to seek and save ALL THAT (i.e., both people and everything else) was lost. Now He has sent you to continue the work.

Let the Supremely Able Helper help you see which Smooth Stones should be in your pouch. Take your Slingshot with you, ready to strike when God directs. Keep developing your skills even as you move along.

Every fight in the world is not yours. Diligently prepare yourself for those that are, and let others focus on the rest.

Danger lurks off the path of your Special Assignment. If you feel like you are losing your way at any point, stop. Ask the Supremely Able Helper for directions. Listen to Him! Stick close to your Partner and He will be right with you every step of the way; you can always count on Him.

Beware of small-minded people who will steal your God-given dream. Mark my words: you will create divine shifts and accomplish great things. I declare it so, not just in general, but in *your* life, David. Now stand up and look out into creation. The way is before you. Go forth, partnering with God to change the world! Fulfill your Destiny!

The End ...

Visit www.TribeofGiantSlayers.com for related resources - and perhaps a little more of the story.

Acknowledgments

Without incredible people like Pastor Bobby Lepinay, "the" Rich Marshall, the Harwoods and Kristina Young, there would be much less to share in these pages. Thank you for your example and encouragement.

Without Pastor Rich Butler, the impact of this project would be substantially less. Thank you for your profound contributions, forward thinking, and significant belief.

Without inspired artwork from Mitch Lehde, and strikingly perseverant editing from J.P. Brooks, the finished product would have paled in comparison to what's here. You are mighty men. Thank you for such unselfish, skilled efforts. Thank you also to the Ulrichs for your creative contributions.

Without my parents and your lifelong appreciation of effective writing, I would never have continued the strenuous climb to better imagery. (Still working on it.) Thank you for everything.

Without you, Sweetheart, there would be no book. Thank you for loving me unconditionally, daring to believe the impossible, creating time for me to write, and the amazing sacrifices you have made.

To my Partner and Guide throughout the writing process, the Supremely Able Helper, we have truly shared rich times together. I look forward to more. There is no one on earth like You.

About the Author

Rick Hubbell has a knack for helping people go beyond discovering their God-given destiny, to actually living it. He's a champion of helping others connect the dots to achieve the great things God has called them to. Neither huge obstacles nor long odds discourage him. He is crazy enough to believe that any Christian can change the world.

In addition to writing and teaching, Rick serves clients around the US as a business growth strategist and an internet marketing specialist. Formerly a full-time pastor at a thriving local church in North Carolina, to Rick's great surprise God called him from there out into the marketplace. The journey to leadership, starting from square one, in both the church and the business world, has given him a distinctive voice of experience. He lives with his wife Jennifer and four children in South Carolina; while his fifth child, Nathan, already lives in Heaven.

Appendices & Resources

A Peculiar Yet Amazing Secret

When I sat down to write this book, I was not certain what it was supposed to be about. No kidding. I only knew that God had told me to write a book, and He had given me the title. Therefore, throughout the process of writing, I made sure to listen closely to the Supremely Able Helper, because if He didn't help me figure it out, I knew I was sunk! But as I asked Him for guidance, listened for His answers, and then obeyed whatever impression or instruction I received. Eventually, over the course of three years, chapter after chapter fell into place.

It was a trying journey of Faith, not the typical 'outline first, then write' experience that my English teacher taught me. One day I'd be working in chapter 4, and the next day I'd be writing a new chapter for much later in the book – a chapter that the previous day I hadn't even known was supposed to exist! However, because I followed this unconventional route, it meant that the book sometimes contained hidden meanings that I myself was not aware of. Let me give you one example.

When I completed the first draft, I wasn't altogether sure why the Supremely Able Helper had inspired me in the first section of the book (Partnering with God) to put so much emphasis on True Identity, Special Assignment, and Partnership with God. These terms - as used in the book - were all new terms to me. From time to time I was also puzzled why the modern slingshot (rather than the kind used in David's day) was the one I felt certain I was supposed to use to help people remember the

Slingshot Principles. But despite my doubts, I obeyed His leading.

Then one day I saw a secret in my own book which I didn't know was there until I was polishing up the final draft. (*Perhaps there are others you can find.*) I observed an odd but striking connection between the Great Entrance to Destiny and the Slingshot, one which bore witness to the foundational connection between the three principles: True Identity, Special Assignment, & Partnership with God. It directly tied Section One of the Book (Partnering with God) to Section Two (Defeating Goliaths).

Remember when we talked about the place where the journeys to know True Identity & Special Assignment come together, and result in the possibility to accelerate in Partnership with God at the Great Entrance to Destiny? I had never realized that this intersection forms a Slingshot shape.

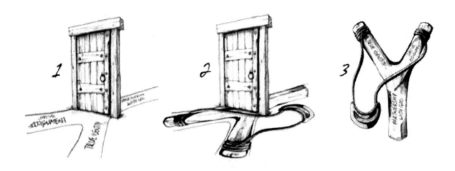

Make of this what you will, but I believe that understanding what is pictured here is important to being able to use the main Slingshot Principles - Prayer, Courage, Skill, and Unconventional Tactics - with much greater effect. It confirms that using the Slingshot Principles with the correct Smooth Stone is a major key to unlocking the Door to Destiny.

I feel it is also important to point out – for those of you who may need this confirmed - that this example shows that the Supremely Able Helper will indeed give you specific ideas and guidance when you ask, that He is indeed much more involved and active and 'speaking' to you - through many different means - than you might have been taught or believed. *"Ask, and you will receive."*

And His ideas lead to great things.

Appendix A

Kingdom Strategy Notes

Many Base Camps pray and speak out using excellent truth and logic about a variety of important things in the everyday world, but too often they fail to send (as in truly commission) their own champions *into* the actual battle. But remember how the Slingshot Principles all work together, David. Effective Prayer, for example, can help you increase your Skill, spark your Courage, and choose the most effective Unconventional Tactics.

The Prayers of Others & the Support of Base Camp

There are many ways to pray; ideally you'll use as many as possible, as regularly as you can. Most important for you personally, of course, are the prayers you pray and the things you learn directly from God while praying. No replacement exists for investing this time with Him. None.

Then there are the prayers of others, which you also need. Some situations are impassable without them, since different kinds of prayer accomplish different things.

Oddly enough though, it's not sufficient for you simply to get together occasionally with a few co-workers, a handful of friends, or even to have a special prayer team. Neither will it work to have big Special Events now and then for this purpose. You might have thought those would get the job done, but they won't: not to the full extent necessary. Maybe you didn't even realize all this Prayer was so important. In truth, David, *you will also need the sustained support of the particularly powerful prayers from your home Base Camp and other Base Camps, and also those from Special Prayer Initiatives which bring many across the body together. Such collective force is earth-shaking.*

If you are going to completely fulfill your Special Assignment, you will need those prayers behind you. We are dependent on each other in the Kingdom of God; that's how the King designed it to function. A great void exists here, which is a major reason it will be impossible for you to take down certain Goliaths until the following basic three part plan is understood. It's not that Base Camps are not praying - many do so regularly and powerfully. It's the limited bandwidth of the prayers.

Let me show you why this is true.

When trying to occupy a major territory with a formidable, deeply entrenched and heavily fortified enemy, does a wise military send in ground troops first and alone? Not usually, not if they want to win. That would be incredibly foolish to send individual soldiers forward unassisted, simply hoping that somehow they can figure out some way to accomplish their objective and eventually make it back to Base for the next meeting.

What does a wise military do instead? First they use longer range weapons to soften up key enemy targets, *then* they send in ground troops. Sometimes the best strategies have different waves which employ different combinations of elements in each wave. It is far easier to approach targets that have already been bombarded by an aerial assault, or by other long range weapons, than to fight them hand-to-hand first.

Can you imagine any wise military suddenly cancelling all air support in the middle of a battle, leaving the ground troops to fend for themselves? Unfortunately, too many Base Camps do not see the need to (1) pray specifically for godly men and women to penetrate the darkness of (for example) the Arts, Media, & Entertainment world, then (2) commission ones the Lord confirms to carry out their Special Assignment there, and (3) keep supporting them in Prayer and equipping them to ensure they reach their objectives.

Here's the effect of that tragic oversight: if your Special Assignment is in the everyday world, as it is for most people (i.e., you're not a traditional missionary, a related non-profit organization, or a full-time Base Camp leader), you miss out tremendously. Actually, so does Base Camp, because if prayers that could help you become more fruitful in your mission were getting prayed, the result would also help your home base!

Once the vision of this simple three-part plan comes alive in more Base Camps, and we all stick with it, amazing divine shifts will begin to occur all over the everyday world. And mark my words David, that time is coming.

CPSIA information can be obtained at www.ICGtesting.com
Printed in the USA
LVOW120137060712

288980LV00004B/1/P